ks *by James L. Christensen*

FUNERAL SERVICES
THE MINISTER'S SERVICE HANDBOOK
HOW TO INCREASE CHURCH ATTENDANCE
THE PASTOR'S COUNSELING HANDBOOK
THE MINISTER'S MARRIAGE HANDBOOK
THE COMPLETE FUNERAL MANUAL

Bo

THE COMPLETE FUNERAL MANU

The Complete

FUNERAL

MANUAL

✠

James L. Christensen

FLEMING H. REVELL COMPANY
WESTWOOD   •   NEW JERSEY

Acknowledgments

Except where identified as King James Version, the Scripture quotations in this publication are from the REVISED STANDARD VERSION OF THE BIBLE, copyrighted 1946 and 1952 by the Division of Christian Education, National Council of Churches, and used by permission. Scripture quotations without references are in the authors own words.

Prayers and comments from THE FUNERAL by Andrew W. Blackwood, Copyright 1942 by the Westminster Press. Used by permission.

Comments from HIGHER HAPPINESS by Ralph Sockman, Abingdon Press, Nashville, Tenn. Used by permission.

Prayers and poems from THE FUNERAL ENCYCLOPEDIA, Edited by Charles L. Wallis. Reprinted by permission of Harper and Row, Publishers.

"The Butterfly" by Alice Freeman Palmer from A MARRIAGE CYCLE. Used by permission of the publisher, Houghton Mifflin Company, Boston, Mass.

The poems "The Rose," by A. L. Frink and "The Two Ships" by Bret Harte are from the booklet MY DUTY by the Clark Grave Vault Company. Used by permission.

The poem "Committal at a Mausoleum" by Chauncey R. Piety is reprinted from THE CHRISTIAN-EVANGELIST, by permission.

The poem from "Renascence." From COLLECTED POEMS, Harper and Row. Copyright 1912, 1940 by Edna St. Vincent Millay. By permission of Norma Millay Ellis.

From COMPLETE POEMS OF ROBERT FROST. Copyright 1934 by Holt, Rinehart and Winston, Inc. Copyright © 1962 by Robert Frost. Reprinted by permission of Holt, Rinehart and Winston, Inc.

Diligent effort has been made to identify authorship and ownership of all other material employed, and so far as the author's knowledge extends, it is all in public domain.

The poems "O Happy Soul" by Washington Gladden and "Mystery" by Jerome B. Bell are from MASTERPIECES OF RELIGIOUS VERSE, ed. by James Dalton Morrison. Used by permission of Harper & Row, Publishers.

The poem "Bees In Amber" by John Oxenham is used by permission of Theo. Oxenham.

DEDICATED
To my paternal grandfather,
James Christensen
who, though dead, lives on—
especially in my thoughts.

Contents

THE COMPLETE FUNERAL MANUAL

I.

The Pastor Ministering Before Death

The degree of a pastor's effectiveness in ministering to those suffering from grief is in direct proportion to his faithful care and counsel of parishioners in pre-death circumstances.

When called to attend the critically ill or to the deathbed, the minister should go at once. Ordinarily he secures permission from the doctor or nurse before calling upon the critically ill, and learns as much as possible about the case, inquiring whether the patient is conscious and whether death appears imminent.

What the pastor says and does depends upon his personal beliefs and the denomination he represents. When speaking to concerned friends who are not Christian, he will probably speak more about Christ and the cross. If the friends are Christian, he will give reassurance about God's love and the future life. If death has already occurred, a ritual of Scripture and prayer may be given in the family's presence.

To the Critically Ill

The pastor may speak a short, simple, hopeful verse of Scripture that could be recalled or memorized. Also, he might write out the verse and leave it with the attending member of the family so that it can be read over and over. Suggested verses follow.

Scripture Sentences

"When I am afraid, I put my trust in thee" (Psalm 56:3).

" 'I will trust, and will not be afraid . . .' " (Isaiah 12:2).

" '. . . in quietness and in trust shall be your strength' " (Isaiah 30:14).

" 'Be still, and know that I am God' " (Psalm 46:10).

"The Lord is my shepherd, I shall not want . . ." (Psalm 23:1).

15

"There is no fear in love, but perfect love casts out fear" (I John 4:18).

"Rejoice in the Lord always; again I will say, Rejoice" (Philippians 4:4).

" 'And whatever you ask in prayer, you will receive, if you have faith' " (Matthew 21:22).

"Bless the Lord, O my soul, and forget not all his benefits . . ." (Psalm 103:2).

"In peace I will both lie down and sleep; for thou alone, O Lord, makest me dwell in safety" (Psalm 4:8).

"We know that in everything God works for good with those who love him . . ." (Romans 8:28).

The pastor also may give a brief prayer concluding each call, providing such will not cause undue alarm or fear. Often the patient will ask for prayer. The pastor should not act hopeless, however near to death the patient may seem.

Pastoral Prayers

Most Merciful Father, look graciously upon Thy servant in *his* distress. Through Jesus Christ cleanse *him* from all sin, visit *him* with Thy salvation, and sustain *him* with Thy tender love. Grant *him* the assurance of the Saviour's presence so that *he* may be led into Thine everlasting light. Into Thy hands we commend *his* keeping, and may Thy peace be over all, through Jesus, the Christ. Amen.

Heavenly Father, take this child of Thine into Thy care tonight. Let no evil come nigh *her*. Be Thou the subject of *her* thoughts, so that when *she* wakes, whether it be in this life or the next, *she* may still be with Thee. Cause *her* to lie down to sleep unafraid in the faith that should *she* not awaken in this life, *she* may rise in the morning of Thine eternal kingdom. And should *she* awake here again, grant that *her* soul may be enlightened by Thy Spirit, through Jesus Christ, Thy Son and our Saviour. Amen.

TO THE BARELY CONSCIOUS

Scripture Sentences

"The Lord is my light and my salvation; whom shall I fear? The Lord is the stronghold of my life; of whom shall I be afraid?" (Psalm 27:1).

" 'Come to me, all who labor and are heavy laden, and I will give you rest' " (Matthew 11:28).

"The Lord is my shepherd. . . . Even though I walk through the valley of the shadow of death, I fear no evil; for thou art with me . . ." (Psalm 23:1,4).

"I sought the Lord, and he answered me, and delivered me from all my fears" (Psalm 34:4).

"Surely goodness and mercy shall follow me all the days of my life . . ." (Psalm 23:6).

Pastoral Prayers

O Lord, our God, Thou dost hold all souls in life and in death. Thou hast spared this our friend through long and gracious years. Receive our thanks for all Thy gifts on *him* bestowed. Grant *him* an entrance into the house not made with hands. There *he* shall serve Thee with powers equal to *his* tasks, through Jesus Christ. Amen.[1]

Wearied by the conflict of life, worn by the burden of the day, we seek Thee as our resting place. May Thine eternal calm descend upon our troubled spirits and give us all Thy peace. Amid the treacherous sands of time Thou standest still, the Rock of Ages. In life's desert place, Thou, O Christ, art a spring whose waters never fail; hear us, we beseech Thee, O Lord, Christ. Amen.[2]

FOR ONE IN A COMA

The pastor should act as though the patient were conscious. There may be no evidence that the person is aware of what is going on about him. Nevertheless, the pastor can never know how much a person in a coma might understand, even when he is unable to respond. The pastor will be careful in what he says to those in the room.

Familiar Scripture and prayer may convey meaning to the subconscious.

Scripture Sentences

"The Lord is my shepherd, I shall not want . . ." (Psalms 23:1).

" 'Blessed are the pure in heart, for they shall see God' " (Matthew 5:8).

" 'Fear not, for I am with you . . .' " (Isaiah 43:5).

" '. . . I will trust, and will not be afraid . . .' " (Isaiah 12:2).

17

" 'Peace I leave with you; my peace I give to you . . .' " (John 14:27).

Pastoral Prayers

Our Heavenly Father, if the time has come for this one to walk through the valley of the shadow of death, we will not fear, for even there Thou art with us. Bring this one at last where Thou art. We are Thine, O God; do with us what seems good in Thy sight. In the name of Jesus, our Friend and Companion. Amen.

O Lord, support us all the day long of this troublous life, until the shadows lengthen and the evening comes, and the busy world is hushed, and our work is done. Then in Thy mercy grant us a safe lodging, and a holy rest, and peace at the last. Through Jesus Christ, our Lord. Amen.[3]

O Thou, Helper when all other help fails, out of the depth of our grief and helplessness we turn unto Thee.

May this one who has been stricken by disease and brought near unto death, realize that Thine arms are around *him*. If, in harmony with Thy merciful purposes, Thou canst raise *him* up and restore *him* in health, our hearts will be filled with joy and thanksgiving. But if Thou dost see it best for *him* to pass into the unseen world, may we be submissive, and may *he* have the consciousness that Thy rod and staff comfort *him* as *he* moves "through the valley of the shadow of death." Grant to *him,* most Merciful Father, that "inheritance, incorruptible, and undefiled, and that fadeth not away." Through Jesus Christ. Amen.

To a "Death-bed Confessor"

If the dying person is aware of his approaching end and asks about God or the "beyond," the pastor may say something like this: "God is your Father; He loves you. Christ is your Friend; He died for you. His cross can save you. His promise is: 'If we confess our sins, he [God] is faithful and just, and will forgive our sins . . .'" (I John 1:9). Do you want me to pray for you?"

Prayer

O God, Thy love was assured to us on the cross; Thy promise to repentant sinners is, "Today Thou shalt be with me in paradise." Grant that promise to this *man* now, as *he* responds to Thy love. In the name of our Saviour, Jesus Christ. Amen.

Then the pastor may have the dying person attempt to say after him, phrase by phrase:

> Just as I am, Thou wilt receive,
> Wilt welcome, pardon, cleanse, relieve;
> Because Thy promise I believe,
> O Lamb of God, I come, I come!

As a benediction, the pastor may say, "Now may the peace of God be yours now and forever. Amen."

If the dying person asks about whether his sins will be forgiven, the pastor may say, "Come now, let us reason together, says the Lord: though your sins are like scarlet, they shall be as white as snow . . ." (Isaiah 1:18). "If we confess our sins, he is faithful and just, and will forgive our sins and cleanse us from all unrighteousness" (I John 1:9). ". . . the blood of Jesus his Son cleanses us from all sin" (I John 1:7). ". . . him who comes to me I will not cast out" (John 6:37).

He may ask the person, "Are you sincerely sorry for the sins that you have confessed, and others that you have committed? Trusting now in Christ and his cross, do you now receive God's pardon and his cleansing grace?"

If the person says "yes," the pastor may ask him to repeat after him: "God be merciful to me, a sinner." He then may offer him the sacraments if he is able to take them.

Pastoral Prayers

Holy Father, here is one of Thy children who needs Thy forgiving love. Look upon *him* in mercy; set *him* free from sin, and prepare *him* for the life with Thee. Through Jesus Christ, our Saviour. Amen.

O Lord, our God, in whose keeping are the issues of life and death: look with mercy upon this our *brother* who lies on this bed of weakness. Grant *him* the grace to repent of *his* sins, and to rest upon Jesus Christ as Saviour and Lord. Amen.

MINISTRY AT THE MOMENT OF DYING

FOR A CHRISTIAN

Scripture Sentences

" 'Father, into thy hands I commit my spirit!' " (Luke 23:46).

" '. . . now lettest thou thy servant depart in peace . . . for mine eyes have seen thy salvation . . .' " (Luke 2:29-30).

" 'Well done, good and faithful servant . . . enter into the joy of your master' " (Matthew 25:21).

". . . the peace of God, which passes all understanding, will keep your hearts and your minds in Christ Jesus" (Philippians 4:7).

" 'He will wipe away every tear from their eyes, and death shall be no more, neither shall there be mourning nor crying nor pain any more, for the former things have passed away' " (Revelation 21:4).

Pastoral Prayers

Depart out of this world, O Christian soul, trusting in the name of God, the Father Almighty, who created thee; in the name of Jesus Christ, who redeemed thee; in the name of the Holy Ghost, who sanctified thee. May thy rest this day (or night) be in peace, and thy dwelling place ever be in the paradise of God. Amen.[4]

O Lord Jesus, who didst weep at the tomb of Lazarus, Thou dost love Thy friends in this family circle. Assure them of Thy presence and comfort in their grief. Show them that Thou art working in all things for their good and Thy glory. Guide them by Thy spirit while they live, then receive them into Thy glory. Through Jesus Christ. Amen.[5]

FOR A NON-CHRISTIAN

Scripture Sentences

" 'For God so loved the world that he gave his only Son, that whoever believes in him should not perish but have eternal life' " (John 3:16).

" 'Believe in the Lord Jesus, and you will be saved . . .' " (Acts 16:31).

"Have mercy on me, O God, according to thy steadfast love; according to thy abundant mercy blot out my transgressions" (Psalm 51:1).

Pastoral Prayer

Merciful Father, who art acquainted with all our ways and who bearest the trials and burdens this one has borne, into Thy judgment we commit his keeping. Whatsoever sins *he* has committed, we implore Thy gracious pardon. Bring to perfections *his* imperfections. We trust Thy mercy, love, and righteousness for the future, and may Thy peace sustain us. Through Jesus Christ. Amen.

MINISTRY IMMEDIATELY FOLLOWING DEATH

On most occasions, the pastor will not be present when death occurs. He will be called from the hospital. Regrettably, he may not be called until after the funeral director has already arrived. Whenever he learns of the death, a call upon the bereaved should take precedence over everything else. He should call immediately.

The minister should speak words of comfort, hope, and assurance. He should allow the bereaved to talk, to express emotions freely, and should never say: "Don't weep"; or "*He* wouldn't want you to cry"; or "Be brave." Crying is a release valve for emotions. The pastor need not say much; the less, the better. Just his presence and strong arm of assurance are helpful.

When the appropriate time seems to have come, the pastor may offer to give a prayer if it has not already been requested.

Pastoral Prayer

For so great a peace we are eternally thankful, our Father. Thou hast been good to us. Wouldst Thou ease our weariness and give us eternal rest. O Thou, who hast brought this one through this earthly journey, may *he* now begin that which is without end, the new life in the new day. We commend *him* unto Thee; in the name of Him who doth bear us up in the hour of our great need, even Jesus Christ, our Lord. Amen.

The minister may offer to telephone relatives, take charge of organizing, or offer advice if it appears needful. In no case should the minister impose upon the funeral director's responsibilities. The minister has charge of only the religious service.

The minister should suggest that he will come back at a later time to discuss the complete funeral arrangement. This will allow the family time to become settled, to be more objective, and to be calm in facing the reality.

If the funeral director is present when the minister calls, however, they may wish to arrive at a mutually agreeable time and place for the funeral service, thus allowing an early press release.

II.

The Pastor's Interview for Making Funeral Arrangements

1.   *Where will the service be held?*

If the deceased has been an active member of a church, it is appropriate for the funeral service to be in the church sanctuary or chapel. Increasingly, church facilities include a chapel for this and other functions, which is designed to accommodate smaller attendances than the sanctuary. The church building is the place where through the years the loyal member has worshipped, been baptized, and perhaps been married. The church contains the symbols of faith and hope. It is fitting for the funeral to be there.

Because a large segment of the population is only nominally associated with a church, or perhaps not at all, the chapel of the mortuary is a suitable and convenient location. Many people consider it inappropriate to take a person's body to a church for a funeral when through his life he avoided the church.

2.   *On what date? At what hour?*

Generally, the practice is to have the funeral service approximately the third day after expiration. This usually allows for the family, however scattered, to be present and for the proper local announcements and arrangements to be made. Occasionally, it is expedient to wait a bit longer, or to have the service earlier.

The time should not be set or announced without the mutual consent of family, funeral director, and presiding minister. Most ministers and funeral homes carry heavily committed schedules which often are difficult to adjust. Each will do his very best to adjust, and all should be consulted before the final decision is made.

Both morning and afternoon hours are acceptable. Usually, the morning hour is 10:00 a.m., and the afternoon, 2:00 or 3:00 p.m. Occasionally there are 4:00 and 5:00 p.m. services.

3.   *What minister will conduct the service?*

If the deceased is a member of a church, then by all means the present minister of the congregation should be asked to conduct the service. It is much better to have only one minister involved in the service in order to retain unity and to carry the pastoral ministry to the family throughout the grief experience.

Occasionally, however, a family may wish to have a former minister participate. From the pastor's ethical code, such is not recommended since the former minister no longer retains pastoral relationships. However, if a family is insistent, then the procedure is to visit with the present minister and request him to contact the former minister, asking him to assist in the service. The assisting minister may read the Scripture and give the pastoral prayer, while the other will give the opening sentences and meditation.

Is there to be music?

The right choice of music can be an affirmation of faith, a spiritual comfort, and a sustainer. The wrong selection, on the other hand, can disturb the emotions, convey morbidness, and confuse theology. Although it is difficult to refuse extreme requests, it is extremely important to choose truly appropriate music for the funeral.

Many services, with increasing frequency, it seems, have only quiet organ music. In many funeral services held in church, the congregation is involved in singing hymns, and the choir in singing anthems, much the same as in a regular worship service. And why not? It is the Christian community offering faith and showing support.

Some services have a soloist or quartet singing.

Some ministers submit a listing of appropriate and recommended selections, both organ and vocal, from which the bereaved may choose. (See list of music in Chapter VII, page 100.)

If the people wish to have expert musicians, who receive remuneration, the funeral director acquires their services. If volunteer talent is acceptable, the minister should offer to contact them.

Is there to be a formal obituary?

The obituary is usually a needless duplication of the biographical facts published in the local press, and a repetition of information that those who attend the funeral service already know. Its use is questionable; hence, in many communities the custom is to have no obituary. Many ministers prefer a brief characterization of the person's life, especially so if he has been exemplary as a person of Christian virtues.

If there is to be an obituary, care should be taken that it not be an exaggerated eulogy, but that it be brief and factual. Some ministers delegate the responsibility of preparing the obituary to some member of the family, with the understanding that he can rewrite or rephrase as necessary. Then, before the obituary is read, the pastor says: "The following statement has been prepared by a member of the family circle"; or "The family has requested the reading of these biographical facts, prepared by a friend of the family."

The obituary should contain the following facts:
1. The full name of the departed.
2. The names of his father and mother.
3. The place and date of his birth.
4. The schools from which he was graduated.
5. The facts about his marriage.
6. The facts about his children.
7. The facts about his life work.
8. The facts about his military service.
9. The facts about his community service.
10. The facts about his fraternal affiliations.
11. The facts about honors, awards, notable achievements, etc.
12. The time and the place of his death.
13. Other factual information that family requests.
14. Those who preceeded and those who are survivors.

Will the casket be closed or open during and following the service?

Increasingly, churches are recommending that the casket not be open at the conclusion or during the funeral service. The religious service for the dead is for the purpose of directing the thoughts and feelings of the bereaved toward the spiritual realities that can sustain the spirit of men in the face of death. The minister, in his witness of faith, hope, and love to comfort the family, will not focus attention on the physical remains of the body, but rather on the reality of the unseen. To present these spiritual values when the attention of the people is fixed on the physical body is a contradiction to the purpose of the religious service. To have the religious service end and then have the casket opened so that the congregation can file past the casket undoes the very thing the minister strives to attain.

It is important, however, for family and friends to look at the dead body to confirm the reality of death and separation which the mind wishes to avoid. One recommendation is that the immediate family view the body for the last time in private prior to the religious service. When the public service is in the afternoon, the viewing by the family may be done in the morning, with the minister leading in a prayer. If the public service is to be in the morning, the prayers and viewing can take place the night before or in the early morning. Thus, the family in private can express and drain off emotions, and be composed for the service of memory. The important psychological values served

24

from seeing the dead body can be satisfied for friends by the body "lying in state" until just prior to the beginning of the religious service. Those who have understood the purposes of the funeral service and have experienced the latter recommendations, testify to their appropriateness and desirability.

Even so, however, the minister and funeral director desire to accommodate the family's wishes within reason.

7. *Is any fraternal order to be present? To take part?*

If the deceased has been a member of a fraternal order, the family may wish the lodge officials to share in the public service. If so, the minister may assent to the family's wishes. If the minister is tactful and considerate, he need anticipate no difficulty in making satisfactory arrangements with the fraternal order. Both the minister and the lodge officials should accede to what the family desires.

If the spokesman of the family is not aware of what is customary, the pastor should explain the possibilities. It is often customary for the lodge to have services on the evening prior to the funeral; hence, it is a completely separate and distinct service. The services are held either in the home, at the funeral parlor, or in the lodge.

Another plan is for the lodge to share with the minister in the formal funeral service. This is done less frequently, because the service becomes too lengthy and there is usually duplication of materials and thoughts.

The preferable and most common place for the fraternal order's participation is at the graveside, providing the short ritual is used. The minister may be asked to give the benediction following the fraternal order's ritual.

8. *What will be the method of disposing of the body—burial or cremation? Is cremation desired?*

Generally, the bereaved will choose burial, either in the family cemetery plot or in the mausoleum. However, cremation is used increasingly in areas where burial plots are at a minimum. Some choose this method because it seems practical, quick, clean, and efficient. To others, cremation helps disengage their focus from the cemetery plot where a loved one may be buried to the spiritual reality and immortality of their loved one. Others choose this method of disposal because they believe it will be less expensive; actually, the cost of cremation is little less, because a casket is required, plus transportation to a crematory.

Both cremation and burial involve oxidation of the body; the former by a rapid process, the latter by a slower one. Some are horrified at the rapid destruction of the physical remains; they consider it an interference with natural processes.

Perhaps the most important consideration in deciding for or against cremation is not the wish of the deceased, but the feelings of the persons who live on. All of us have "body consciousness," or a "body image." We have many feelings about our own bodies. When we think about the death of someone dear to us, the "body image" is involved— we identify emotionally. We tend to feel sensations that the deceased is now incapable of feeling. For example, we tend to cringe a bit at the thought of a corpse being dissected, or of burning, or of intolerable injury. This is the reason why many choose the casket and vault —because it gives them a sense of protection for their loved one. If the survivors feel this way, they should not choose cremation.

The Christian concept is that the body during the earthly life is a temple of God's Spirit. So, by whatever method of disposal, the body after death is to be treated with reverence and dignity, not as something worthless.

Cremation usually takes place after the public funeral service. Occasionally, however, cremation takes place first, then the memorial service is held, followed by interment of the ashes. Interment is usually in a columbarium provided by the city or cemetery company. Occasionally, relatives will want to scatter the ashes of their loved one among properties that were dear to him, or scenes of childhood. The funeral director will make all arrangements necessary, if a cremation is desired.

In Chapter IX (page 137) are committal materials for the mausoleum and columbarium, as well as for the graveside. If memorial services are desired following cremation or burial, suggested meditations are found in Chapter V (page 58).

9. *Where will the interment take place? Is it to be public or private?*
If the interment is to be in another city some distance away, it may be impossible for the minister to go. In that event, perhaps an assistant may be able to go, or in some cases arrangements can be made for a minister in the distant city to accommodate the family. However, it is time well spent as a servant of Christ if the minister can find the time to fulfill this important part of his ministry to the family.

The same essential materials, by and large, will be used whether interment is private or public. Though always brief, the length of this part of the service will be governed a great deal by the weather.

10. *Will this be a military service?*
There are three possible plans for conducting a military funeral

service. The first is the formal "chapel service," where full honors are afforded, including band, military escorts, caisson, and colors. If the civilian clergyman is asked to conduct such a service, he should consult a chaplain or the military person in charge of arranging the details, who will be informed as to what procedures are appropriate. The body of the deceased will have a military escort who will assist the family and participants in the service, and be ready counsel to the minister. Periodically, the various branches of the military publish manuals, which include detailed instructions regarding military honors and conduct at funerals. For example, the Mortuary Affairs Department of the Air Force published in July 1965, *Air Force Manual*, 143–1. Other branches of the service have similar information. A chaplain of the appropriate branch of service will cooperate in loaning such resources.

A second plan is for a military procession at the cemetery entrance to the grave following religious services elsewhere. In such a procession, the following order is prescribed: band, military escort, colors, clergy, caisson or hearse and casket bearers, caparisoned horse if the deceased had been mounted, honorary pallbearers, family, members of patriotic or fraternal organizations, and friends. After the bearers have deposited the casket on the descending device and the religious committal service has been read, the flag is removed from the casket and held in horizontal position waist high during the benediction, the appointed squad fires three volleys of blank cartridges, the bugler plays taps, and the flag is folded and presented to the closest kin. Then the soldiers march from the grave, and the family is dismissed.

The third plan for a military service includes the flag-covered casket, the presence of military casket bearers, the firing squad, and the playing of taps at the graveside. The rest of the service is the same as any regular service.

11. *Is there any other suggestion about the service?*

Frequently, families will have favorite portions of Scripture or a favorite poem they want read, or will request special seating arrangements.

12. *Is there to be a memorial cause to which friends might be encouraged to give?*

Members of the family often wish for persons to contribute to enduring causes, such as: the cancer society (if one died of cancer), the heart fund, the church (especially if the deceased was actively involved), community service agencies, etc.

If there is to be such a fund, it should be decided early enough so

27

that the announcement can be made with the obituary item in the local press. Friends should be instructed where to send their checks, and who will be custodian of the fund until it is sent to the recipient. Care should be taken that the words "in lieu of flowers" are never used.

13. *Is there anything else that the church can do?*
This is a time when families should feel free to let others help, and it is a unique opportunity for the church. Some possibilities are: assigning someone to answer the telephone or the doorbell, making a car available for errands, providing a baby sitter or child care, providing accommodations for out-of-town visitors, finding persons to take over chores in the kitchen, providing a room at the church for the large family to eat on the day of the funeral, providing food during the period when so many relatives and friends come, and providing pallbearers.

14. *Does the family know how to reach the minister?*
The family may wish to contact the minister to correct or add to the information which he has received. After thinking about the questions asked, often the original decisions are changed. The minister needs to be available.

15. *Is there any special request before we pray?*
The interview should be closed with a prayer for the bereaved. Asking this question affords a convenient way to bring the interview to a conclusion and to suggest the prayer without embarrassment to any family member. It is appropriate to ask all in the house to join hands in a circle, thus eliminating distracting conversations and binding the family by close ties of mutual loss and support. A suggested appropriate prayer is the following.

Heavenly Father, from whom we have come and unto whom we all must return: Thou alone dost understand the sense of loss which has been sustained by these dear people. Into Thy care we commit them. We would not have Thee remove their grief, but ask that Thou bind up their broken hearts with faith and an awareness of Thy presence. Sustain them in these hours. May their loss not seem more real than the gain that has come to their beloved. We pray in the name of Him who said, "Because I live, you, too, shall live." Amen.

PERMANENT RECORD FORM FOR CHURCH AND PASTOR

Full Name of Deceased _____
Age _____

Address _____

Time and Place of Death _____

Church Membership _____

Names of Parents _____

Name of Wife or Husband _____

Names and Addresses of Children _____

Funeral Time, Date, and Place _____

Funeral Home in Charge _____

Order of Service _____

Scriptures Used _____

Meditation Title _____

Interment Place _____

Other Information _____

Officiating Minister(s) _____

III.

Explanations of Haunting Questions

The bereaved almost always have questions and doubts which haunt them. Frequently the minister is approached for an answer. It is a difficult assignment for a minister because there are no definite, proven answers to much of the curiosity regarding death. Our knowledge is limited. The Christian religion is one of faith, not scientific proof. Also, people in grief are not emotionally ready for a deep, complex, theological discourse. Viewpoints among Christians vary greatly. Nevertheless, part of the pastor's ministry is to give as affirmative and satisfying answers as possible, consistent with Biblical revelation. In some areas it is well to confess that "we do not know."

I am aware of the inadequacy of attempted written answers and of the variety of viewpoints; nevertheless, the following attempts may become helpful explanations for some pastors in this important ministry. They are designed to be used as starters for meditations, as well.

Does a person survive his body?

Sir Oliver Lodge is quoted as saying that smashing an organ is not equivalent to killing the organist, nor is killing the organist equivalent to stopping music. The fact seems to be that the body is transmissive, it transmits one's personality; it is the instrument for our expression. For example, the body you see is not totally your mother, nor the most real part of your mother.

Chancellor Arthur Compton, Nobel Prize winner in the field of physics, says, "It seems that the fact of free will demands that our thinking be partially independent of brain activity, a conclusion which suggests . . . the possibility of consciousness after death!"

In the process of growth, biological scientists say that every cell in the body—including brain cells—changes every seven years. In the course of 70 years, a person will have used up nearly ten bodies, yet individuality and memory persist. Personality survives the bodily changes. Is it not possible that personality survives the bodily change of death?

30

Man is not just a physical creature. He can be analyzed into chemical constituents worth several hundred dollars. However, this doesn't tell the whole story, because man has self-consciousness, freedom, reason, awareness of values, memory, a sense of the infinite and self-transcendence. These are the marks of human personality, and are unexplainable on a material hypothesis.

More and more psychologists and scientists affirm that there is something about man that is capable of functioning without limitation of the physical body, and is potentially able to survive beyond death. For example, the self is able to observe itself, judge itself, guide and shape itself. We can get outside of ourself, look down at ourself, and reflect about ourself.

Dr. William Ernest Hocking explained that he believed each of us has an "excursive self" and a "reflective self." The excursive self is our physical, temporal, limited self that moves about in the world, mingling with people, gaining knowledge. However, behind the scenes, initiating these activities, subjecting them to critical examination, and guiding them is the reflective self. It is the reflective self that possesses continuity and transcendence.

Is immortality reasonable?

Hunger could never have persisted without food. Man breathes, and the universe provides air. Men seek for knowledge, and it is provided.

Wherever a human function has persisted, unwearied by time, uncrushed by disappointment, rising to noblest use in the noblest of persons—that function corresponds to some reality. This is man's experience. It is unthinkable that God would create persons with the ability of hunger and thirst, without providing the means to satisfy the appetite.

Men have always dreamed about, yearned for, and believed in a future life beyond this veil of flesh. Surely the capacity for such was not of man's making, nor his own mental projection. The fact that we seek for wholeness and fulfillment surely means that God has provided for the reality, to satisfy the human hunger for immortality.

Whenever I am tempted to doubt the reality of life after death, I ask myself how God could have led me to live for eternal things, only to let death annihilate everything. If God is dependable and just, He would not have placed the song of heaven in my heart unless there is heaven; He would not have awakened me to an awareness of eternity if there is no eternity.

31

Surely, God, who made us in His image, who has permitted us to develop into self-conscious persons who dream dreams of life that has no end, would not terminate our growth or snuff us out as one blows out a candle. Just as it's unthinkable for a draftsman to spend sixty years building a fine, intricate watch, and then crush it to bits in a few short hours, so it is unthinkable that God would perfect a mind like Plato's, a soul like Shakespeare's, or a spirit like St. Francis', only to throw them away like leaves blown by the wind.

How unintelligible and cruel of God it would be, if this life were all there is!

Isn't immortality beyond human experience?

Before coming into this world, each of us was an unborn baby. In going from this world into another one, we are still unborn babies so far as that other world is concerned. If a baby not yet born, still tucked under his mother's heart, could think, he might say to himself, "This is a wonderful place. It's warm. I'm fed. I'm taken care of. I'm secure. This is a great world where I now am. I like it." And then someone might say to him, "But you're not going to stay here. You have to move on. You're going to die out of this place. You're going into another world." That baby would look upon the process of birth as if it were death, since it would be the end of the pleasant state he was in. And he would protest, "I don't want to die. I understand it here and feel secure. I want to stay." What to us is birth, to him is death, and he resists it. But the day comes when he does die to that life, and is born into our world.

What happens to him? He is cradled in loving arms. Soft hands hold him gently. A kind face looks down at him, and he loves that face. Everybody who comes near loves him. He is the king of the world he surveys. Then he begins to grow, and he finds life good. Oh, he has some struggles and hardships, but that is to make a man of him. He has some difficulties, but he loves God and people love him. And he loves this world, with its seasons, its beauty, its human companionship.

Finally, he gets to be an old man and he is told, "You have to die." He protests, "I don't want to die. I love this world. I like to feel the sun on my face, and the cool rain. I like our dear, human ways. I love the faces of my wife and children. I've lived here a long time. I don't want to die." But he does die to this world, and is born into the next.

Can we believe that all of a sudden the character of God and the constitution of the universe are going to be changed so that the person will be born into a place of gloom and terror, or will be left in a state of nothingness? That is preposterous!

He will awaken to find himself young again. Loving faces will greet him; loving hands will touch him. More beautiful sunlight will surround him; sweeter music will sound in his ears. All tears will be wiped from his eyes, and he will say, "Why was I so afraid of this thing called death, when as I now know, it is life?"[1]

Cling to this conviction of the goodness of God, and believe that your dear one has gone, not into darkness, but into light. Think of death as a rainbow bridge which all our departed loved ones have crossed and which we too will cross one day to be reunited with them.

What kind of body will we have?

Paul the Apostle says, "If there is a physical body, there is also a spiritual body" (I Corinthians 15:44). God gives us earthly bodies for the first phase of our lives, just as He gives us our first baby teeth. When the baby teeth are no longer useful, or are too small or decayed, they come out and second teeth come in. These earthly bodies are useful for awhile; then they are replaced by "spiritual bodies," or glorified bodies.

Paul says the difference between a natural body and a spiritual body is somewhat like the difference in the seed, the stalk, and the flower of a plant. The life of the plant lives first in the seed, then in another body—the stalk, and finally in a third kind of body—the flower. So it is with us. We live for a time in our natural bodies until they grow too old or get too sick for us to live in them any longer. Then we live in our "spiritual bodies," which will do for our spirits in the stage beyond what our flesh-and-blood bodies do here.

In the future we will not be "floating wraiths," but real people. Our bodies will be tools for our spirits, just as Jesus after the resurrection had a body that was able to function. Jesus transcended the ordinary limits of space and time and matter, and lived in a form of existence that was higher than the earthly. This is a demonstration of the continued and more glorious life which is possible for us. ". . . in Christ shall all be made alive" (I Corinthians 15:22).

Will we know one another?

The Disciples were able to recognize Jesus in His spiritual body. After the resurrection, He appeared on numerous occasions to approximately 500 different people. Though He was not confined to a physical form, yet He was recognizable. They saw the scars in His hands and feet. Thomas knelt down in awe, declaring, "My Lord, my God."

When we say the creedal article "I believe in the resurrection of the body," we actually are saying that we believe in a principle of identity. Paul, in using the phrase "resurrection of the body" surely did not mean the body we now have. The body we now have is designed in its function for earth. A change in gravity would make our bone structure obsolete. Who would want to drag around the body of flesh we now have through eternity? Furthermore, how could mutilated, diseased, amputated, or cremated bodies be recovered?

Believing in the "resurrection of the body" means that personality will not be lost, and each will have an individual "spiritual body." Our physical bodies are the means of identity. We locate our friends as distinct individuals because they have bodies. So in the future we still will be separate "somebodies," with spiritual bodies. The New Testament Greek had no word for "personality." Linking "spiritual" to "body" may be an ingenious expression for what we mean by "personality."

A kernel of wheat produces a wheat stalk, never a corn stalk. A rose root will produce only a rose. Just so, our unique self will be known and recognizable. Just as surely as we know one another on earth by our natural bodies, so we shall be known by our spiritual bodies in the future realm.

What about multiple marriages in the heareafter?

This is essentially the controversy that the Sadducees brought to Jesus, as recorded in Mark 12:18–25. The Sadducees, who did not believe in the resurrection, wanted to present the matter in the most unfavorable light possible, so they cited the case of a woman who had been married to seven brothers one after another, all of whom had died. Intending to make survival after death ridiculous, they asked, "In the resurrection, whose wife will she be?" Jesus answered, ". . . when they rise from the dead, they neither marry nor are given in marriage, but are like angels in heaven."

This does not mean that there will be no personal relationship whatsoever in the after-life, but it will not be the continuation of troublesome earthly entanglements or physical ties. The relationships there will be those of mutual spiritual kinships.

Perhaps Jesus' definition of "family" will help our understanding. One scene in Scripture pictures Jesus in the synagogue teaching the people (Matthew 12:46–50). His brothers and mother, who did not always understand Him, were in the audience. Apparently a bit embarrassed by His claims and subtle challenges which tramped upon the dignitaries' toes, they concluded that He was beside himself. In an attempt to save the situation, they summoned the "head usher" to slip up and whisper to Him, "Your mother and your brothers are outside. They must speak to you." This was the occasion when Jesus asked, "Who is my mother and who are my brothers?" Pointing in the direction of His Disciples, He said, "Here are my mother and my brothers! For whoever does the will of my Father in heaven is my brother, and sister, and mother."

Actually, we belong to two families: one is by blood ties, the other is spiritual kinship. Our physical family may or may not be a part of our spiritual family. We are accustomed to think that the closest relationships are those bound by ties of blood. However, Jesus' teaching indicates that there is a bond closer than blood. Our most congenial, meaningful associations are spiritual and psychological affinity. If one has intimate rapport, deep understanding, and genuine love with a mate, it is because they have developed a spiritual kinship. True love involves a soul, a heart, a mind, and a will, and is a convergence and blending of these. Where the latter is absent, there is no abiding relationship beyond death in spite of marriage. If marriage is only a physical attraction or convenience, love will diminish when the body diminishes. But there is a spiritual bond stronger than the bond of flesh, an eternal bond far surer than the death-broken bonds of time.

The relationships that will be real, abiding, and meaningful in the hereafter are those in which we have mutual spiritual kinships.

Is there a heaven and a hell?

Dr. Ralph Sockman has said, "The more I study the gospels, the more I think of our passage to the next life as through a schoolroom rather than a courtroom." Eternal life is an extension of the courses we have taken here. A person will carry over into the world on the other side of death the qualities which he has developed here. Death will not arrest one's progress. God gives a chance to go on, but He does not change the rules of the school.

With this view, the world is an elementary school in which the first lessons of love, truth, and beauty are learned; it is an antechamber to the vast university of eternity, in which there are many colleges and schools for those who have reached different degrees of faith and holiness.

Death is progress in whatever direction we are pointed. If we have not learned much of good in this life, we shall have to start the next without much of good. If we have not learned to like what Christ liked, we will be miserable. Those inclined toward God will rise closer to Him—"God Himself shall be with them." This will be heavenly. We will know, "for now we see in a mirror dimly, but then face to face."

Those inclined away from God will be taken by death even farther away from Him. That is the awful state that Jesus called "outer darkness."

Sin is violation of love, even more than law. That is why a broken heart is worse than a broken leg, and a frustrated love is harder to bear than a severe burn. That is why "hell" can be described as spiritual agony—the ashes of loneliness, the fires of remorse, the tediousness of frustration, the emptiness of separation, the burning shame of being shown what we really are.

Kenneth Foreman pictures a new arrival in heaven who was asked, "What would you like to be up here?" The soul answered with great enthusiasm, "I want to be a saint in glory." The questioner looked dubious. "What experience have you had?" he asked.

We are supposed to be getting some practice and experience now for our future. Our finest joys are dim foreshadowings of what is to come. The loves of earth are authentic samples of the love of heaven. Those we have loved in this world will mean far more to us than they ever have before. The finest marriages and families give a dim foretaste of what the loves of heaven will be like. Every year heaven seems less strange. Everyone we love who goes there makes it more like home, and makes us look forward to our reunion. "Enoch walked with God, and he was not, for God took him." He just walked on with a Friend whom he had come to know and to trust.

Can we describe heaven?

The Bible says, "What no eye has seen, nor ear heard, nor the heart of man conceived, what God has prepared for those who love him . . ." (I Corinthians 2:9). In other words, we human beings have no complete conception of heaven, only intimations and attempted descriptions of its glory.

If unhatched chicks were able to talk through their shells, and if we were to learn their language, how much could we tell them about the life they will be having? Very little, because their experience would be so limited and confined.

We tend to ask for detailed and specific descriptions of the heavenly life, and we must confess that the realm lies beyond the bounds of our reason, experience, or information. Christians have often spoiled the attractiveness of heaven by presumptuously trying to know more about it than the Bible tells. The Bible tells us enough to satisfy our needs, but perhaps not enough to satisfy our curiosity.

We must be careful not to materialize or literalize the descriptions we do have. If we were to describe the balmy, sunlit climate of southern California to an Eskimo who had never been away from the snow and ice of northern Alaska, how would we do it? Well, we might tell the Eskimo that southern California is a place where there is no ice or snow, no midnight sun, no whale meat. This would tell us something. However, this would tell very little positively about southern California.

Similarly, in trying to preview the hereafter, the author of the Book of Revelation resorts to negative intimations: "There will be no night there, no tears, no dying . . . no more pain. . . ."

In writing of heavenly things, he does not say that they are "thus" and "so," but only that they are *like* this or that. He takes the most precious things of earth, and uses them as symbols of spiritual truth. He takes the most beautiful things he has seen, the jasper and the emerald, the rainbow and the sea, and declares that what he envisions in heaven is "like" these things. They are the least inadequate comparisons he knows to employ to suggest something which is ineffably wonderful.

In the same faith, Paul looked forward to "what no eye has seen, nor ear heard, nor the heart of man conceived, (namely) what God has prepared for those who love him."

Where is heaven or hell?

Is heaven here on this planet? Or on another planet? Is hell deep inside the earth?

The locations cannot be geographically pinpointed. The distance cannot be measured in feet or miles, because these are physical categories of time and space; apparently, the future realm is not limited to these categories as we know them.

In a sense, it is like trying to explain "How wide is electricity?" We can measure the voltage and strength of an electric current, and we know fairly accurately the speed of electricity. We also know the reality of electricity, for we need only to unscrew an electric bulb and put our finger in the socket. Nevertheless, electricity has no breadth, length, height, or weight so far as we can know.

Neither can one explain in literal dimensions the location and size of heaven or hell. These are spiritual conditions. Heaven is where God is and where He is loved and respected. The Bible mentions various beings, such as angels, being in heaven. Hell is the opposite; it is where God's wishes are not respected.

It is impossible for us to understand this, for we associate life with physical bodies and death with dead bodies, and places by geographic locations. However, Jesus intimated that one can enter the Kingdom of Heaven without waiting for earthly death. I presume that one can experience hell before physical death as well.

Will we go immediately to heaven?

Our "time concepts" seem not to apply beyond this world. Perhaps that is why there is no clear answer to such questions as, "Do the souls of the departed go immediately to heaven, or do they wait for a resurrection of the dead?" Jesus said to the dying thief, "Today you will be with me in Paradise," but He also said to a believer, "I will raise him at the last day."

Some have tried to reconcile this by the theory of the soul being asleep and dormant until the resurrection day. Because they have been unconscious in the interval, it will seem that they have gone straight from death to the awakening.

Others believe that the souls of the redeemed and the lost go at once to their final destinations, but remain in a sort of interim state until they are reunited with their bodies on the judgment day.

Neither of these explanations is completely satisfying. They try to impose our time concept on another realm. The question "When do we go into God's presence?" may be an absurdity before Him in whose sight a "thousand years are but as yesterday when it passed" (KJV). As soon as the faithful die, we can think of them as already in heaven.

Is heaven desirable?

Mark Twain said that something he disliked was almost as bad as "being damned to John Bunyan's heaven."

We often make heaven seem horribly boring or cloyingly sweet, thus spoiling its attractiveness.

The Bible says that the dead "rest from their labors" (Revelation 14:13), but it also says that the heavenly beings keep so busy praising God that they "rest not day and night" (Revelation 4:8, KJV).

Most of mankind has always been tired, so the prospect of an eternity of rest from labor has been a heaven to look forward to. Hence, heaven has been pictured as a place of rest. Jesus bade people

"Come to me, all who labor and are heavy laden, and I will give you rest" (Matthew 11:28).

To be sure, rest from labor is an important part of our picture of heaven, but perhaps to "lie down for an aeon or two," as Rudyard Kipling put it, will suffice in that regard. And then "the Master of all good workmen shall set us to work anew."

People now have enough leisure to get enthusiastic about the joys of labor. This has encouraged a dissatisfaction with the prospect of eternal rest. The concept of heaven as a place of perpetual harps and crowns and rest becomes intolerable to the activist. As one minister said, "I would be impelled to cry, 'Move on,' to any saints who persisted in playing their harps under my window for a million years." Most of us desire to know what there will be to do. Rest assured, it will not be all idleness.

The occupations of the world to come are unkown. It can be noted, however, that man on earth strives for infinite and unachievable ideals. Beyond the frustrations of this life, there will be further opportunity to come closer to those gleaming summits. If this is true, then the life beyond will not be a thing of monotony and stagnation, but of continued progress and achievement.

What difference did Jesus make?

Christianity has had a profound influence upon belief about death and immortality. One of the imperative needs of the Christian church today is to understand and teach the concepts of the future life as revealed by Jesus Christ, who "brought life and immortality to light through the gospel" (II Timothy 1:10).

A great many funeral inscriptions have been collected from the ancient non-Christian Roman Empire. Some of the actual epitaphs recovered by the archeologists are: "I was; I am not; I do not care"; "What I have eaten and what I have drunk, that is all that belongs to me"; "While I lived, I drank willingly; drink, ye who live"; "Eat, drink, play, come hither." Such are some of the typical expressions of the materialism, hedonism, and cynicism which prevailed in the ancient Roman Empire. Behind these flippant words was an empty vulgarness of life, and a disbelief in immortality.

Immortality was the Greek idea. Plato set forth the belief that man is not only a body but also a soul (*pneuma*), and the soul by its very nature is indestructible by forces that kill the body. It was the Greek idea that the soul lives apart from the body.

Resurrection of the body, which is a different thing than mere

39

immortality, was a Hebrew view. The Hebrew made no sharp distinction between the body and the soul as did the Greeks. The Hebrews anticipated the raising of the whole person (the body) in the life beyond. However, in Jesus' time, the Jews were greatly divided in their opinions about this theory. The Sadducees denied the resurrection, while the Pharisees believed in it.

Jesus' unique contribution was to confirm the resurrection, not only in His teaching, but by His own post-death appearance. He was raised, to be seen on eleven different occasions by at least 500 different people. It was not the resurrection of the "physical body," but a glorified, spiritual body. He said, "Because I live, you shall live also."

It was this "demonstration" and clarifying of the issue which caused Paul to say to the Thessalonian Christians, "Do not grieve as others who have no hope." That the Christians actually did have an utterly different attitude from the hopeless cynicism of the Romans, the vague mysticism of the Greeks, and the confusion of the Hebrews, is made unmistakable by their own funeral inscriptions. Many have been preserved in the catacombs at Rome, where we read: "Mayest thou live in the Lord Jesus"; "Thou wilt live in God"; "Thou wilt live forever."

Is death God's will?

Too readily, it seems, we respond to untimely, hard-to-understand tragedies by saying, "Well, I must accept it. It is the will of God."

And, to be sure, in the wisdom of God, He did design death. ". . . it is appointed for men to die once . . ." (Hebrews 9:27). When a baby is born, one thing we know for certain—sometime death will come to that person. Death is the termination of this earthly life.

However, the time that death comes involves many human factors, and cannot be attributed always to God. Jesus once said, ". . . it is not the will of your Father which is in heaven, that one of these little ones should perish" (Matthew 18:14, KJV). Not all deaths can be blamed upon God.

Dr. Leslie Weatherhead, in a little book entitled *The Will of God,* makes this plain by dividing the subject into: the intentional will of God; the circumstantial will of God; the ultimate will of God.

He illustrates his thinking with the death of Jesus, God's unique Son. Was it God's original intention that Jesus should die on a cross? It was God's intention, says Dr. Weatherhead, for men to follow Him and thus be redeemed. The *discipleship* of men was the intentional will of God.

However, when circumstances wrought by men's evil set up such

40

a dilemma that Christ was compelled either to die or to run away, then in those circumstances the cross was the will of God. It was God's circumstantial will. A father in the evil circumstances of war might say to his son, "It was never my intention that you be a soldier. I have always dreamed of your being a teacher, but under the prevailing circumstances, I want you to assume the responsibility." There are human elements which often cut short human life, contrary to God's ideal purpose and intention.

However, in spite of all the evil circumstances and heartbreak, God ultimately accomplishes His intentional will. This is the hope which sustains us. God's original purposes cannot finally be defeated. God was able to use even the circumstances of the cross to fulfill the redemption of man by raising Jesus from the dead.

Not all that happens is God's will, but nothing that happens can ultimately defeat His will.

This is why we say, "In His Will is our peace"; and why we pray, "Not my will, but Thine be done."

Why has death happened?

God's purpose in creation was to develop personalities. He has provided four factors for the development of persons. In the intermesh of these factors, explains Harry Emerson Fosdick, "comes good, but also there comes sorrow."

The first factor is a world of order, where natural law operates. They are orderly, dependable laws which hold the universe together. They are intended for good, but when they are disregarded or not considered, or when men have not learned to utilize or control them properly, they cause disaster. The law of gravity, which allows our livelihood on this planet, may tomorrow, if violated, pull an airplane to destruction. We would not want a universe without law; it is necessary for good. Yet, it causes much tragedy.

Another factor is that God created for us an unfinished world. ". . . the whole creation groaneth and travaileth in pain together until now" (Romans 8:22, KJV). We are called upon to cooperate with God in completing the universe. It is a struggle to overcome ignorance, disease, poverty, war, and physical obstacles. Human suffering is often the incentive for stimulating research and humanity's progress.

The third factor is that God has given man freedom. The only way a person could develop and become good is by conscious choice; from this comes much misery, sin, and tragedy. We choose what we shall do, and inevitably some choices are unwise and sinful. Hence, there

41

are human elements in much of the tragedy produced by man's misuse of freedom. To respect man's freedom, there are some things God cannot do without making man a puppet and Himself a dictator.

The final factor is the inter-social relations. We do not live in a vacuum, but with others. The evil men do spills over into other people's lives. We are bound together, and that communal relationship brings sorrow. We are part of a family, sharing the benefits and progress of those who have gone before, but we also share the risks and liabilities. If a football team makes a touchdown, and, in the process, one of the players is hurt, he does not say it is unjust. It is part of the game. So it is with the human family.

Everything worthwhile springs from these four factors. Yet, from these also come our tragedies.

IV.

Meditations for Various Circumstances

DEATH IN FULL AGE

(For an Older Person)

"You shall come to your grave in ripe old age, as a shock of grain comes up to the threshing floor in its season" (Job 5:26).

There is something good and glorious in the death of an aged person. Death appears more natural and appropriate, less an intrusion and shock, than when it comes to a child, or youth, or one middle-aged, burdened with responsibilities.

"Length of days" was thought to be a peculiar and cherished blessing promised to Abraham, David, Job, and untold millions. Who among us does not agree? Why else do we strive to prolong life?

Long life multiplies the opportunities for service in glorifying God. When a person's life is prematurely cut short, what a shame! I am thinking of Raphael, the artist, who died in his thirties; of Jesus Christ, who was murdered at the age of thirty-three; of thousands of military boys, whose lives have been snuffed out in young adulthood; of children, whose potentials never had a chance to blossom. What tragedy! How unfortunate! What loss to the world! What a privilege to live to full age. Think of the mature judgment, usefulness, and labor of many years. Think of the accomplishments of those in sunset years.

Titian painted his masterpiece "The Battle of Lapanto" at the age of 98, Verdi wrote his great opera *Otello* at 74, and *Falstaff* at 80. Kant, at 74, wrote his anthropology; Edison built chemical plants after he was 67; General MacArthur was Supreme Commander of the occupation in Japan in his 70's. Socrates learned to play a musical instrument in his old age; Canto, at 80, studied Greek; Plutarch, almost as old, studied Latin. Dr. Samuel Johnson applied himself to the Dutch language only a few years before his death; yet one morning in later life, he amused himself by committing to memory 800 lines of *Virgil*; at the age of 73, while suffering from an attack of paralysis

43

so severe that it rendered him speechless, he composed a Latin prayer in order to test the condition of his mental facilities. Chaucer's *Canterbury Tales* were the composition of his later years. They were begun in his 47th year and finished in his 61st. Franklin's *Philosophical Pursuits* began when he had nearly reached his 50th year. Sir Christopher Wren retired from public life at 86; after that he spent five years in literary, astronomical, and religious pursuits. Necker offers a beautiful instance of the influence of late studies in life when he tells us, "The era of three scores and ten is an agreeable age for writing; your mind has not lost its vigor, and envy leaves you in peace."

As mature, ripened corn is snatched from the withering stalk of autumn's frost, so the spirit sheds those parts which are no longer of value in the environment which is being entered.

Shortly before his death, Edward Madison Cameron delivered a lecture to his aging body: "When you can go no further, I shall leave you and be free . . . when we separate I shall continue to exist. . . . A Power greater than you and I started us on our journey. Your journey is approaching its end and you are aware of it. . . . My journey has merely begun, and I know it because I have never been more alive. Our separation is therefore not one of sadness, but of joy. You are weary and want to stop. I am longing to alight from this slowing vehicle and go on without you."

THE GREAT TRANSFORMATION

(For a Cancer Victim)

"We know that we have passed out of death into life . . ." (I John 3:14).

Cecil B. DeMille, the renowned movie director of world fame was also a man of Christian faith. It was he who first dramatically depicted the Biblical stories on the screen. Shortly before his death, he wrote the following.

"One day as I was lying in a canoe, a big black beetle came out of the water and climbed up into the canoe. I watched it idly for some time. Under the heat of the sun, the beetle proceeded to die. Then a strange thing happened. His glistening black shell cracked all the way down his back. Out of it came a shapeless mass, quickly transformed into beautiful, brilliantly colored life. As I watched in fascination, there gradually unfolded iridescent wings from which the sunlight flashed a thousand colors. The wings spread wide, as if in worship of the sun. The blue-green body took shape. Before my eyes had

44

occurred a metamorphosis—the transformation of a hideous beetle into a gorgeous dragonfly, which started dipping and soaring over the water. But the body it had left behind still clung to my canoe. I had witnessed what seemed to me a miracle. Out of the mud had come a beautiful new life.

"And the thought came to me," continued Mr. DeMille, "that if the Creator works such wonders with the lowliest of creatures, what may not be in store for the human spirit?"

Death is the shedding of those parts which are no longer of value in the new life being entered. Yet putting them aside in no way disturbs, threatens, nor destroys the future expression of our total being. We are but set free from the old, and will be given a new body to glorify God.

Dwight L. Moody is reported to have said to a group of friends, "Some morning you will read in the papers that D. L. Moody is dead. Don't believe a word of it! At that moment I shall be more alive than I am now. I was born of the flesh in 1837; I was born of the Spirit in 1856. That which is born of the flesh may die; that which is born of the Spirit shall live forever."

NUMBERED DAYS

(For a Heart Attack Victim)

"For everything there is a season, and a time for every matter under heaven:

> a time to be born, and a time to die;
> a time to plant, and a time to pluck up what is planted;
> a time to kill, and a time to heal;
> a time to break down, and a time to build up;
> a time to weep, and a time to laugh;
> a time to mourn, and a time to dance;
> a time to cast away stones, and a time to gather stones together;
> a time to embrace, and a time to refrain from embracing;
> a time to seek, and a time to lose;
> a time to keep, and a time to cast away;
> a time to rend, and a time to sew;
> a time to keep silence, and a time to speak;
> a time to love . . ." (Ecclesiastes 3:1–8).

Paul Tillich, the late, distinguished theologian, has given us a definition of time: "Time is our destiny. Time is our hope. Time is our

45

despair. Time is the mirror in which we see eternity." Indeed, the way we use our life determines our destiny; it is our hope or our despair, and reflects in advance our eternity.

Longfellow's perception was, "Time is the life of the soul."

The Psalmist knew it as well, which is why he penned, "So teach us to number our days that we may get a heart of wisdom" (Psalm 90:12).

In the light of this sudden death, let us remember the admonition, "Number your days."

Life is brief at its longest. "As for man, his days are like grass; he flourishes like a flower of the field; for the wind passes over it, and it is gone, and its place knows it no more" (Psalm 103:15–16); "Do not boast about tomorrow, for you do not know what a day may bring forth" (Proverbs 27:1).

It is the knowledge that our days are limited which makes each one precious. Let us not presume upon the tomorrows so that we are unfit for life today. "Give us this day, our daily bread. . . ." Let us fill each day with the quality of eternity. Let us live the moment before us to please God, and trust the future without fear.

The *New York Times,* several years ago, printed the story of a Swiss who observed his eightieth birthday by taking stock of his life with the aid of an unusually detailed diary. He looked at himself statistically. He figured that he had spent 26 years, 312 days, and 18 hours sleeping; 21 years, 85 days working; 5 years, 346 days being angry; 302 days waiting for people with whom he had appointments; 5 years, 346 days eating; 228 days shaving; 26 days scolding the children; 12 days, 16 hours lighting cigars or cigarettes; he had laughed only 1 day, 22 hours.

The omissions from the tabulation tell as much as the inclusions. There is nothing about worship, reading, meditation, or serving. One is prompted to ask, "Eighty years on earth for what?"

In the World War II motion picture *Bridge Over the River Kwai,* amid the dark loneliness of the enemy-infested Thailand jungle, the guard of the bridge converses with himself as he paces back and forth: "How have I used the years at my disposal? Have I accomplished anything of note and worth? Has the world been better for my having lived?" This was deep calling unto deep. These are questions worthy of our reflection.

> If I had time to sit myself down
> Full face to face,

46

With my better self that does not show
In the daily life that rushes so,
I might be struck by the thought sublime
If I had the time.[1]

"So teach us to number our days." Why? "That we may get a heart of wisdom" (Psalm 90:12).

Only he who realizes the value of his days will have the wisdom to fill them with quality.

Only he who knows that each day is a precious gift from God will have the wisdom to use his days as responsible to God.

Only he who sees each day as opportunity for spiritual growth and expression will have the wisdom to practice the presence and develop the relationship that will never die.

Only he who discerns the eternal nature of time will have the wisdom to invest his life in unselfish, enduring service.

We live in deeds, not years; in thoughts, not breaths;
In feelings, not in figures on a dial.
We should count time by heart-throbs. He most lives
Who thinks most, feels the noblest, acts the best.[2]

Quality of life is more important than quantity. "How" one lives is more important than "how long" one lives. Jesus lived usefully and meaningfully in a mere thirty-three years on earth.

One day a mother said in disgust at a prank of her young son, "Mike, for heaven's sake, what on earth are you doing?"

She asked better than she knew, for it is relevant to us all, "What *on earth* are you doing *for heaven's* sake?"

THE GAIN IN DYING

(For a Middle-Aged Person)

The Apostle Paul made a strangely true statement, "For me to live is Christ, and to die is gain." Could death ever be thought of as gain? Such a conclusion sounds like that of a sick mind. However, think more deeply about it. As Charles Kingsley suggested:

Death is gain when it means the end of sorrow, terminates all the diseases of one's body, the errors of one's mind, the imperfections of one's character, and the stains of sinful living.

Death is gain when it delivers one from the imperfections of the present state, introduces one into the scenes and services of immor-

47

tality, unites one with the society of the "just made perfect," and gives one the honor of serving God without weariness or end.

Death is gain if it kills no part of us save that which hinders us from perfect life.

Death is gain if it raises in a moment from darkness into light, from weakness into strength, from sinfulness into holiness.

Death is gain if it perfects our faith by sight, and lets us behold Him in whom we have believed.

Death is gain if it gives us to those whom we have loved and lost, for whom we have lived, and for whom we long to live again.

Death is gain if it joins a child to the mother who has gone before.

Death is gain if it rids us of doubts and fear, of change and chance, of space and time, and of all which space and time bring forth and then destroy.

Death is gain, for Christ has conquered death, for Himself, and for those who trust Him.

The assurance of such gain for you and all men is to live as Christ. The secret of assurance of future gain lies in present living. How eternal your life will be is dependent upon how much of the eternal Christ you have in your heart. It is all yours *if* you are Christ's.

"He that hath the Son, hath eternal life. He that hath not the Son, hath not eternal life."

A young widow wrote to her pastor. Her husband had just died, and she was left to care for three small children. This is what she said in her letter:

As I looked out of my window last night, I saw the moon shining in the heavens, and I thought about it shining on my husband's grave. For a moment I was lonesome. But then I thought: "No, he isn't there." The next day my six-year-old boy came home from school. He fairly burst into the house, excited because of what he had to tell me. He said, "Mother, just think! Daddy has seen Jesus now!" I thought to myself, "Yes, Son, how true! And he has seen Peter and Paul and Martin Luther, and John."

God's Graduates

(For a Young Person)

When one graduates from one grade to another, or from one school to another, whether it be from junior high to high school, or from high school to college, there is always a tinge of sadness about the conclusion of years which, in retrospect, appear more valuable and wonderful than ever. However, the exercises that come at the end of school are never called a program of ending; it is customary to call them a "commencement."

This is exactly what death is like. Dr. Ralph Sockman says, "The more I study the gospels, the more I come to believe that we pass from this life to the next by way of a schoolroom rather than by way of a courtroom. Eternal life is the extension of the courses we take here. God gives us another chance, but He does not change the rules of the school."[3] Death is commencement in Christ's school. We are met to honor one of God's graduates.

For this young person, death has meant a transition from the terrestrial to the transcendent. It has meant an emergence to another of the successive levels of existence, just as were the various graduations to the levels of a career in education.

Jesus at one time said to His disciples: "No longer do I call you servants, for the servant does not know what his master is doing; but I have called you friends, for all that I have heard from my Father I have made known to you" (John 15:15).

They began to follow Him as seekers. They were attracted to His teaching, swept along by the crowds, and shared the longing for what He had to give. They wanted what He had to offer. This was the first level of discipleship.

Finally, they graduated to the second stage in the relationship. They advanced from mere seekers to servants of Christ. At first they sought what Christ could do for them, but continued until they asked what they could do for Him.

The third stage was that of friendship. In His farewell discourse, recorded in John 15, Jesus said, "No longer do I call you servants . . . but I have called you friends. . . ."

To be a friend is to have a warm, intimate understanding and confidence, which a servant does not know. It is to be in complete accord in all things, joined with affection and good will. When we children of God graduate into true friendship with God, we open infinite new possibilities of experience.

Horace Bushnell so lived and loved His way into understanding friendship with God that it was said that even his dying was play to him.

"Enoch walked with God . . . and then he was not, for God took him."

PEACE FOR THE DISTRESSED

(For a Suicide)

The gospels record the incident of the disciples sailing upon the beautiful Sea of Galilee. The Master was asleep when suddenly a storm descended upon the lake, causing the waves to almost swallow up the tossing, rocking, rolling ship. Frantic and fearful beyond control, the disciples awakened Jesus, pleading, "Master, save us or we perish!" Calmly He said, "Peace be still," and the sea was calm. Even the elements obeyed His will, and human spirits were quieted, and fretted nerves were calm in His presence.

It was He who promised, "Peace I leave with you; my peace I give to you; not as the world gives do I give to you. Let not your hearts be troubled, neither let them be afraid" (John 14:27).

Oh, how many have found in the midst of their troubled spirits an infinite calm, a peace of soul that has carried them through the storms of life. That inward peace can be yours today.

First, peace of mind can be found in recalling the good qualities of_____'s life. There was so much that was commendable, high principled, genuine, and compassionate. It could be illustrated by each of you, in your associations with this one.

The Apostle Paul gave us sound advice when he admonished, "Whatever is true, whatever is honorable, whatever is just, whatever is pure, whatever is lovely, whatever is gracious, if there is any excellence, if there is anything worthy of praise, think about these things" (Philippians 4:8). The sense of distinct pride in this one's achievements makes the loss more profound, but in this recollection also is experienced peace of mind. In the words of the Apostle Paul to his friend, Philemon, may we say, "I thank my God always when I remember you . . ." (Philemon 1:4).

We also find a peace of mind in the realization that this death has brought rest and release from deep mental distress and inward suffering. We do not know the reasons for the death. It is not our duty individually to condone or renounce, to pronounce judgment or censure. God alone understands.

Death is usually caused by physical accident or disease; this one has been caused by emotional factors—a sickness as real as organic illness. None of us has ever faced such a crisis of personality. Apparently *he* was driven helplessly to escape what evidently seemed to *him* an unbearable existence. For many, the termination of flesh is the way the troubled mind can be put at ease. Perhaps this seemed welcome release from the frustrations and disappointments of life. Death is nature's merciful provision to terminate earthly life. Let us assume that this untimely death was the result of an irresistable urge to find peace from that which was emotionally troublesome. In this assumption, may we find comfort.

Likewise, you may find a peace of mind in the reassurance of the resurrection. That the human spirit lives beyond physical death is a basic affirmation of the Christian faith. The resurrection of Jesus is the keystone of our faith. It was verified by historical witnesses which put it beyond the realm of human doubt. The Master said, ". . . I am the resurrection and the life; he who believes in me, though he die, yet shall he live, and whoever lives and believes in me shall never die . . . (John 11:25).

It Is Well!

(For a Child)

In the 4th chapter of II Kings is recorded a heart-rending story of a Shunammite woman whose only son died while sitting upon her lap. Her first action was to go see God's prophet, Elisha. The first question he asked her was, "Is it well with the child?" He wanted her to focus attention on the child.

This should be *our* first concern, as well. So much of our sorrow at time of death is self-pity. We think of our own loss and the pain in our own hearts which separation brings. We are too self-centered; our thoughts turn inward.

We should try to forget *our* circumstances, and consider "Is it well with the child?" If we knew that the child were safe, and well, and happy, then we could be consoled, and could face the future without despair.

The mother in the Biblical scene came by faith to the realization and conviction "It is well" with the child. Though broken-hearted and disappointed by her loss, yet based upon her knowledge of God, she was *assured* of the child's welfare.

Jesus took children in His arms, blessed them, and said, "Of such is the Kingdom of God."

Everyone knows that Jesus is right. There can be no doubt about it. Whatever else remains that is questionable or uncertain, this rings true: "Of such is the Kingdom of God." Our Lord says it. We all feel in our hearts that these words are true.

We have learned how God can pack heaven into a small bundle of life. We have held eternity in our arms. We have recognized something that will never die, a soul radiant with heaven. If heaven is of such life as this—and we have our Lord's word that it is—then we have good reason to be comforted.

When a child goes to heaven, one of the strongest, yet most delicate, ties on earth is broken; but in our loss God creates another tie, all

51

the lovelier and stronger because He has promised that nothing can ever break it. You have loved your child. Well, heaven is like that. Your affections have been environed in heavenly things as you have loved your child.

Does not heaven come nearer now because *his* soul is there? Do not grieve for *him*. You can trust God's merciful provisions, abundantly more wonderful than anything we know here. "What no eye has seen, nor ear heard, nor the heart of man conceived, what God has prepared for those who love him . . ." (I Corinthians 2:9). The child's new world is better than this earth, for it is a home of goodness and love. It is safe, lasting, secure, and removed from peril. *He* is:

> Safe in the arms of Jesus
> Safe on his gentle breast.

Remember also that this child will be spared the sorrows, sins, and stains of earth. *He* will never know the risks of infirmity. *He* ". . . shall hunger no more, neither thirst any more; the sun shall not strike them, nor any scorching heat. For the Lamb in the midst of the throne will be their shepherd, and he will guide them to springs of living water; and God will wipe away every tear from their eyes" (Revelation 7:16, 17).

ANGEL UNAWARE

(For a Small Child)

Psalm 127:3, 4: Lo, children ". . . are a heritage from the Lord, the fruit of the womb a reward. Like arrows in the hand of a warrior are the sons of one's youth."

Kahlil Gibran amplifies the thought: "Your children are not your children. . . . They came through you but not from you. And though they are with you yet they belong not to you . . . you may house their bodies but not the souls, for their souls dwell in the house of tomorrow, which you cannot visit, not even in your dreams . . . you are bows from which your children as living arrows are sent. . . . Let your bending in the archer's hand be for gladness; for ever as He loves the arrow that flies, so He loves also the bow that is stable."

This child was loaned to you by the Heavenly Father. You have been blessed of God with the privilege of parenthood. What joy the child has brought to your hearts. "My soul magnifies the Lord, and my spirit rejoices in God my Savior . . . for he who is mighty has done great things for me, and holy is his name" (Luke 1:46–49).

For reasons unknown to us, the child returns to the One who gave it. ". . . the Lord gave, and the Lord has taken away; blessed be the name of the Lord" (Job 1:21).

Edgar Guest gives the words of comfort and faith which we need for such a loss. He has God say:

> "I'll lend you for a little while,
> A child of mine," he said.
> "For you to love the while he lives,
> And mourn, when he is dead.
> It may be six or seven years, or 22 or 3,
> But will you until I call him back,
> Take care of him for me?
> He'll bring his charms to gladden you,
> And should his day be brief,
> You'll have his lovely memories
> As solace for your grief.
> I cannot promise he will stay,
> Since all from earth return,
> But there are lessons taught down there,
> I want this child to learn.
> I've looked this wide world over
> In my search for teachers true
> And from the throngs that crowd life's lanes,
> I have selected you.
> Now, will you give him all your love,
> Nor think the labor vain,
> Nor hate me when I come to call,
> To take him back again?"
> I fancy that I heard them say,
> "Dear Lord, thy will be done.
> For all the joy thy child shall bring,
> The risk of grief we'll run,
> We will shelter him with tenderness
> We will love him while we may,
> And for the happiness we have known,
> Forever grateful stay.
> But should the angels call for him,
> Much sooner than we have planned,
> We will brave the bitter grief
> That comes and try to understand."[4]

SAY IT WITH FLOWERS

(For an Infant)

We do not understand the reason nor the mystery of this infant's death. However, we are assured that:

> It was not in cruelty,
> It was not in wrath,
> The reaper came this way:
> But an angel visited the green earth
> And took the flower away.[5]

How interesting is the comparison of a flower and a baby; let us consider a *lily* and a *baby*.

A lily is one of the most beautiful of the products of the earth—how queenly white, how symmetrical, how pure. So is a child—lovely in form, angelic in complexion, beautiful in color, and smooth of skin.

Lilies are delicate, tender, and susceptible to disease, with little endurance. Some flowers have more endurance. Others are perennials. But the lily is short-lived. To be enjoyed by the owner, to add beauty and attractiveness to her home, the lily must be plucked early.

> The flowers of spring have come and gone.
> The blossom of an hour
> My summer flower has passed away
> My autumn trees look cold and bare.[6]

"My beloved has gone down to his garden . . . to gather lilies" (Song of Solomon 6:2).

Nevertheless, every flower has a mission. No blossom blooms in vain. Every opening blossom, though brief its span, sheds fragrance which blesses, gladdens, sweetens, and beautifies the world. Each in its sphere makes its little life a blessing.

Though this loved one is removed at a tender age, you parents will never be the same in character. This little life has brought you closer, made you richer, moved you deeper than anyone could ever have done. To have planned for and felt the warmth and love of such a child's fragrance, even for a brief span, leaves your spirits gentler and sweeter. You have entered a new world from which you can never depart.

As John Watson has written, "No little child has ever come from God and stayed a brief while, returning again to the Father, without making glad the home, and leaving behind some trace of heaven.

The family would count themselves poorer without those quaint sayings, those cunning caresses, that soft touch, that sudden smile. This short visit was not an incident; it was a benediction."[7]

So this child has fulfilled a God-appointed purpose.

TRANSPLANTED TO GOD'S GARDEN

(For a Premature Baby)

Sometimes a seed is sown in a flower bed in which it is only permitted to germinate and leaf, but not to blossom and unfold. Then it is transplanted to another place, to evade the wintry storms and fierce winds. There it is watched with tender hands, warmed with sunshine's rays, nourished carefully, and permitted to blossom into its full beauty.

So it is often with babies. As early removed flowering plants, they are transplanted to God's garden, to receive His special care, to grow in the field of paradise, and to add beauty to heaven's realm.

> And the mother gave in tears and pain,
> The flowers she most did love.
> She knew she could not find them all again,
> In the fields of light above.[8]

YOU SHALL BE COMFORTED

(For General Use)

"Comfort, comfort my people, says your God. Speak tenderly to Jerusalem . . ." (Isaiah 40:1, 2). There is comfort available to the anguished in heart.

Paul, in his letter to the Corinthian church, wrote, "Blessed be the God and Father of our Lord Jesus Christ, the Father of mercies and God of all comfort, who comforts us in all our affliction, so that we may be able to comfort those who are in any affliction, with the comfort with which we ourselves are comforted by God. For as we share abundantly in Christ's sufferings, so through Christ we share abundantly in comfort too" (II Corinthians 1:3–5).

You who have experienced the death of your loved one can be helped to face your loss, and to assimilate it into your life that must go on.

You will be comforted somewhat by expressing your feelings freely.

In our society, some seem to put a premium upon a stoical containment of emotion, hence they repress any expression of feeling. Such only delays the reaction, or causes unwholesome results.

Tears are an escape valve for the welling up of all kinds of emotions that are normal and acceptable.

This ceremony is for the purpose of providing an atmosphere for mourning the death of someone near and dear. We are to talk about your loved one, to remember your associations together, to relive those times, to re-think *his* meaning to you, to re-thank God for *his* remembrance, and to weep if you feel like it. A person is more than a physical body; therefore, our reasons for appreciation go beyond physical dimensions, to the qualities of spirit, the attitudes of mind, and the essence of soul. To believe in man is to believe in God, in whose likeness he is made; contrariwise, to believe in God is to believe in man's infinite worth. We, as friends, have come in this ceremonial way to express with you, our emotions of grief. "Blessed are those who mourn," said Jesus, "for they *shall* be comforted" (Matthew 5:4).

You will also be comforted by the supporting fellowship of relatives and friends. Death leaves us so lonely. It is like a curtain of separation which is hard to bear. In the anguish and distress, you may be tempted to withdraw.

However, the best antidote is the love of relatives, neighbors, friends, and brothers and sisters in Christ. One of the most striking customs that was ever brought to this country was the "Irish wake." Friends and relatives of the deceased would sit up through the night and day, reminiscing about the life of the one who had died. This sharing of loss knit them close together, giving supportive, positive help to the bereaved.

We affirm today by our attendance that we are one family in God. We convey our empathy, and enter into the loss you have sustained to provide a protective layer of love. One lady who faced this ordeal of grief said, "I could have never made it without my friends."

Again, you may be comforted by the consolation of religious beliefs.

When you do seem to come to the end of human assistance, remember that the invisible companionship of the Heavenly Father is always with you. "Though I walk through the valley of the shadow of death, I will fear no evil, for thou art with me. . . . Underneath are the everlasting arms. . . ."

There is comfort in the knowledge of God's everlastingness. "Lord, thou hast been our dwelling place in all generations. Before the mountains were brought forth, or ever thou hadst formed the earth and the world, from everlasting to everlasting thou art God" (Psalm 90:1, 2).

Change and decay in all around I see,
Oh Thou, who changest not,
Abide with me.[9]

There is comfort in the knowledge of God's forgiveness. ". . . though your sins be as scarlet, they shall be as white as snow . . ." (Isaiah 1:18, KJV).

There is comfort in the knowledge of God's empathy. "In all our afflictions, he is afflicted. He is touched with a feeling of our infirmatives."

There is comfort in the assurance of God's power which raised Jesus from the dead. "Let not your hearts be troubled; believe in God . . ." (John 14:1). Put your trust in God, who in His wisdom brought this life into being, and who will guide its future destiny.

O light that followest all my way,
I yield my flickering torch to Thee,
My heart restores its borrowed ray,
That in Thy sunshine's blaze its day
May brighter, fairer be.
O Cross that liftest up my head,
I dare not ask to fly from Thee,
I lay in dust life's glory dead,
And from the ground there blossoms red
Life that shall endless be.[10]

Amen.

V.

Memorial Meditations

Memorial services are usually held with no casket present, and following the interment of the deceased. More often than not, the service will be held in the church sanctuary of the deceased; hence, it should be triumphant in mood.

The memorial meditation should usually contain personal references to the deceased, speaking appreciation for *his* or *her* life and contributions, yet witnessing to the faith triumphant and the resources of God to assuage grief.

THE NOBLENESS OF HOME-MAKING

(For a Mother and Home-Maker)

Someone has said, "The three most beautiful words of the English language are Home, Heaven, and Mother." It is no accident that the three are linked, because they are closely related. That which makes home heavenly is a devoted mother in it; and that which will make heaven like home is a mother in it.

We come to honor one of time's most honored occupations, that of home-making. Have you ever noticed how often Jesus couched the language of the Kingdom in the metaphor of the home and family? Apparently, He felt that the home relationships of father, mother, sister, and brother were the essence of Kingdom relationships.

We are met to pay tribute to an exemplary home-maker, who has been recognized as such by family, community, and friends. Perhaps her life can best be characterized by the author of Proverbs 31, who expressed the extraordinary qualities of such a woman in relationship to her husband, her household, and her world:

A good wife who can find? She is far more precious than jewels. The heart of her husband trusts in her, and he will have no lack of gain. She does him good, and not harm, all the days of her life. . . . She opens her hand to the poor, and reaches out her hands to the needy. . . . Strength and dignity are her clothing. . . . She opens her mouth with wisdom, and the teaching of kindness is on her tongue. She looks well to the ways of her household, and does not eat the bread of idleness. Her children rise up and call her blessed; her husband also, and he praises her: "Many women have done excellently, but you surpass them all." Charm is deceitful, and beauty is vain, but a woman who fears the Lord is to be praised. Give her of the fruit of her hands, and let her works praise her in the gates. (Proverbs 31:10–12, 20, 25–31)

How fittingly beautiful to think of her death as did the composer who wrote: "Goin' home . . . I'm just goin' home. It's not far: Jes' close by, through an open door."

Here on earth we dwell in one room of our Father's house. But this room does not exact the magnitude or marvel of the Father's great house. In His house there are many rooms. The earth is one room; there is yet another prepared beyond that. Dying is going on into that other room. Since it is the Father's house, this is home-going, rather than going into a strange and fearsome place.

How do you recognize your home? Well, in many ways. However, few of us do it by determining the architecture or the color of the house. Instead, we have feelings of familiarity and of the presence of loved ones, which cause us to say: "This is where I belong. This is where I can be myself. This is home." As much as our earthly room seems home to us, it is not complete. Our real dwelling is with God, where our Heavenly Father is known face to face. This is home.

In our existence on earth we are much like children born of American parents on foreign land: we know we are Americans, we speak the American language, we wear American clothes; but we have never seen our native land. We have studied its geography and its economic and political institutions, and have heard of its fabulous luxury and beauty. We know that we have only to present ourselves at its gate to be welcomed as members of the family, but we have never actually lived there. We want to go home, to our home, someday; we wonder what it will be like. Others have gone on ahead of us. Finally, the time comes. We are excited about it! We look forward to it! We pass under the Golden Gate Bridge, and, lo, it is more beautiful and fabulous than we have ever been told. This is our homeland. So it must be with the heavenly home.

About a hundred years ago, the Reverend John Todd was a noted New England minister. When he was a very small boy, his mother and father died within a short time of each other; and he was brought up by an aunt. He was educated at Yale, and eventually became the pastor of the Congregational Church in Pittsfield, Massachusetts.

One day he received a letter from his aged aunt. She had been told by her doctor that she was afflicted with a grave disease from which she was not likely to recover. She wrote a pathetic letter to her distinguished nephew, asking for some word of comfort from one better educated and more richly experienced than she herself.

As he could not go to see her immediately, John Todd wrote her a letter, which happily has been preserved. This is what is written in the letter:

It is now thirty-five years since I, a little boy of six, was left quite alone in the world. You sent me word that you would give me a home and be a kind mother to me. I have never forgotten the day when I made the long journey from my home to yours. I can still recall my disappointment when I learned that, instead of coming for me yourself, you had sent your colored man, Caesar, to fetch me. I can still remember my tears as, perched on your horse and clinging tight to Caesar, I started for my new home. Night fell before we finished the journey and as the darkness deepened, I began to be afraid. "Do you think she'll go to bed before we get there?" I asked Caesar anxiously. "Oh, no!" he replied. "She'll sure stay up for you. When we gets out of these 'ere woods, you'll see 'er candle right enough."

Presently we rode into a clearing, and there, sure enough, I did see a friendly candle in the window. I remember that you were waiting at the door, that you put your arms around me, that you lifted me—a tired and bewildered little boy—down from the horse. There was a bright fire on your hearth, a warm supper on your stove. After supper, you took me up to my room, heard me say my prayers, then sat beside me till I fell asleep.

You are probably wondering why I am now recalling all this to your mind. Someday God will send for you, to take you to your messenger of death. At the end of the road, you will find love and a welcome; you will be safe in God's care and keeping. God can be trusted—trusted to be as kind to you, as you were to me, so many years ago.[1]

The Towering Greatness of a Man of God

(For an Elder of the Church)

In describing King Saul long ago, the author of the Book of Samuel (I Samuel 9:2) described him in these words: ". . . from his shoulders and upward he was higher than any of the people" (KJV). Saul could be picked out of a crowd because he towered above them all. He was head and shoulders above the rest.

Not because of physical stature, like Saul, but rather because of his spiritual stature, like Paul, _Charlie_ and was a man that stood head and shoulders above the rest.

Though his life has spoken its own testimony and needs no added word from me, yet we could not let this date pass without speaking the tribute we all feel and know. Merely to enumerate some of his qualities becomes an encouragement to us. We come here as neighbors, friends, and loved ones in great admiration for the faith, judgment, leadership, character, and service of this man of God.

He towered head and shoulders above the crowd level in *civic service*. If the greatest among men are the servants, then this man stands tall because he gave of himself unselfishly in leading civic organizations and in personal helpfulness. He befriended many a businessman, youth, and student. He walked the streets of this city and beyond in errands of service, leaving "footprints in the sands of time."

He towered head and shoulders above the crowd level as a *churchman*. The church was the center of his busy life. He served this congregation in nearly every conceivable capacity, and was looked up to as an elder statesman of insight, gracious spirit, broad sympathy, sound judgment, faithful stewardship, and fairness. When one reads Paul's catalogue of qualifications for an elder, he sees how closely this man fulfilled them all. An elder ". . . must be blameless; he must not be arrogant or quick-tempered or a drunkard or violent or greedy for gain, but hospitable, a lover of goodness, master of himself, upright, holy, and self-controlled; he must hold firm to the sure word . . ." (Titus 1:7–9). All of this could be said of our brother because of his churchmanship, love of ministers, and devotion to God through Christ.

Last, but not least, he towered head and shoulders above the crowd level in *personal character*. He was an image of a saintly gentleman: trustworthy, kind, compassionate, understanding. Isaiah said of such, ". . . they shall call them, The holy people, The redeemed of the Lord . . ." (Isaiah 62:12, KJV).

He was undoubtedly a lover and admirer of the Apostle Paul. One of his favorite Scriptures was II Timothy 4:7–8: "I have fought the good fight, I have finished the race, I have kept the faith. Henceforth there is laid up for me the crown of righteousness . . . not only to me but also to all who have loved his appearing." A man like this shall receive "a crown of glory that fadeth not away" (I Peter 5:4, KJV). Undoubtedly, he has been exalted to the "realm of the redeemed." This is his victory day.

> He is not dead, he hurried on
> Ahead of us to greet the dawn,

That he might meet the beloved who left
Us yesterday. We are bereft—

But weep not. Hail him where, afar,
He waits for us on some bright star.

He is not dead. Beyond all strife,
At last he wins the prize of life.[2]

Robert Milliken, the great scientist, paused one day in his room and reflected upon the great scientific age in which we live and the meaning of it all; and he wrote, "The divine architect of the universe has not built a stairway that leads to nowhere." From our congregation he has gone to take his place in God's larger assembly of saints.

Ten thousand times ten thousand,
    In sparkling raiment bright,
The armies of the ransomed saints
    Throng up the steeps of light;
'Tis finished, all is finished,
    Their fight with death and sin;
Fling open wide the golden gates,
    And let the victors in.[3]

OPENER OF NEW WORLDS

(For a Schoolteacher)

Teaching is an honorable profession. Jesus, our Master, was primarily a Teacher. When Nicodemus, the distinguished member of the Jewish "Supreme Court," paid the Master a visit, he gave Jesus one of the highest compliments the Jews knew to give: "Master, we know you are a teacher sent from God, for no man can do the things that you do except God be with him." To His pupils He often asked: "Do you not yet perceive or understand? Are your hearts hardened? Having eyes do you not see, and having ears do you not hear?" (Mark 8:17–18). It was His responsibility to get the message "in."

We pay our earnest respect and appreciation for this one, who has influenced so many youngsters both in and out of classrooms. What love, patience, understanding, self-control, empathy, tact, wisdom, moral integrity, and faith are required to be an effective teacher.

William L. Sullivan, in his writing *Epigrams and Criticisms in Miniature,* says: "How much easier it is to write a ton of books on pedagogy than to produce one teacher of sensitive structure, noble manner, and fine taste, whose essential presence and inward habits are a constant dissuasive to vulgarity and a living recommendation of the beauty of learning and the dignity of wisdom."

A child who sits in a class directed by such a teacher is exposed to the finest influence possible. Thank God for such teachers. Contrariwise, James wrote: "Let not many of you become teachers . . ."; he knew that a teacher's effects last eternally. Opening new worlds and vistas to the mind, and helping to develop a child mentally, physically, and spiritually are no little responsibilities.

Henry Adams wrote: "A parent gives life, but as a parent, gives no more. A murderer takes life, but his deed stops there. A teacher affects eternity; he can never tell where his influence stops."

Daniel Webster's classic words are appropriate: "If we work upon marble, it will perish. If we work upon brass, time will efface it. But if we work upon men's immortal minds, if we imbue them with high principles, with the just fear of God and love of their fellowmen, we engrave on those tablets, something which no time can efface, and which will brighten and brighten to all eternity."

BUILDING A TEMPLE

A builder builded a temple,
 He wrought it with grace and skill;
Pillars and groins and arches
 All fashioned to work his will.
Men said, as they saw its beauty,
 "It shall never know decay.
Great is thy skill, O builder:
 Thy fame shall endure for aye."

A teacher builded a temple
 With loving and infinite care,
Planning each arch with patience,
 Laying each stone with prayer.
None praised her unceasing efforts,
 None knew of her wondrous plan;
For the temple the teacher builded
 Was unseen by the eyes of man.

Gone is the builder's temple,
 Crumbled into the dust;
Low lies each stately pillar,
 Food for consuming rust.

63

But the temple the teacher builded
Will last while the ages roll,
For that beautiful unseen temple
Is a child's immortal soul.
                    —*Author Unknown*

It is because of our mutual appreciation and admiration for _____
as a teacher who manifested a Christian spirit and dedication, that
we lift up the teaching profession as a tribute, and challenge some
among *her* pupils to follow this noble calling.

One first-grade teacher shares her enthusiasm for the work: "When
I'm introduced as a teacher, I am usually asked what I teach. When
I say, 'First grade,' I usually hear a flat, 'Oh.' I've never been certain
whether it is an expression of pity, sympathy, disgust, or perhaps dis-
interest. Always, I wish I had the time to explain to them like this:

'Yes, I teach the first grade. Where else would a handsome and very
young man put his arms around me and ask, "Did you know that
I love you?" Where else could I wear the same dress day after day
and be told each time that it is pretty? Where else could I walk up and
down aisles and have one little hand touch me? Where else could I
have the privilege of wiggling loose teeth and receive a promise that
I can pull them when they are loose enough? Where else could I eat
a soiled piece of candy from a little grimy hand and not become ill?
I have to eat it because he is watching to see that I do. Where else
could I guide the first letter formation of a chubby little hand that
may someday write a book or an important document? Where else
could I forget taxes and even the state of the nation because Stevie
isn't grasping reading as he should and other methods must be tried?
Where else would my mind have to stay so young as with the group
whose attention span is so short that I must always keep a bag of
tricks up my sleeve? Yes, I do teach the first grade, Mr. and Mrs.
America, and I love it.' "[4]

THE GREAT HARVEST

(For a Farmer)

We have met to honor a farmer of good reputation, _____.
Farmers have been the life lines of the American economy. They are
the caretakers of God's earth, co-workers with Him in its produce.
What a glorious privilege to be a farmer!

How Jesus must have loved country folk. So many of His parables
elude to the imagery of the farm: "A farmer went out to sow . . . some

seeds fell on rocky ground, where they had not much soil . . . other seeds fell upon thorns, and the thorns grew up and choked them. Other seeds fell on good soil and brought forth grain, some a hundredfold, some sixty, some thirty. . . ."

He knew the frustrations and joys of agriculture. Nevertheless, He commended and loved responsible farmers who accepted the management of the soil, as a trusteeship from God!

However, He told about one farmer whose greed and materialism led to self-centered living, pursuit of hilarious pleasure, self-righteousness, hoarding in the midst of human need, and a false sense of security. "What shall I do, for I have nowhere to store my crops?" said the farmer of good fortune. "I will build larger barns . . . I will store all my grain. . . . Then I will say to my soul, 'Soul, you have much goods laid up for many years. Eat, drink, and be merry.' Jesus said to him, "Thou fool! This night thy soul shall be required of thee." Blessed is the farmer who recognizes his dependence upon God, and uses the earth's produce in responsible stewardship.

John Burroughs testified that he had been saved by "good, hard work on the farm with his hands, raking and hoeing, plowing and planting, feeling the good earth between his fingers . . . feeling his oneness with the universe." The plow, he said, had done its perfect work on him, as in the fields. "The bitterness and boredom had been plowed under; the stagnant pools of discontent drained off."

The one whom we honor had developed this relationship with God, and found an enrichment of soul.

WHO MAKES A GARDEN

Whoever makes a garden
Has never worked alone,
The rain has always found it
The sun has always known.

The wind has blown across it
And helped to scatter seeds.
Whoever makes a garden
Has all the help he needs.

Whoever makes a garden
Should surely not complain,
With someone like the sunshine
And someone like the rain.

And someone like the breezes
To aid him in his toil
And someone like the Father
Who gave the garden soil.

Whoever makes a garden
Has, oh, so many friends;
The glory of the morning,
The dew when daylight ends.

For wind and rain and sunshine
And dew and fertile sod
And he who makes a garden
Work hand in hand with God.[5]
        —*Douglas Mollock*

Many of the Biblical metaphors affirming our faith in the resurrection and future life use farm terminology. Though today's agriculture is far different from that of the ancient past, yet these descriptions are not beyond our appreciation. The mystery of a wheat crop may be beyond our understanding, but it is not beyond our experience.

The Apostle Paul said: "What you sow does not come to life unless it dies . . . what you sow is not the body which is to be, but a bare kernel, perhaps of wheat or of some other grain. But God gives it a body as he has chosen, and to each kind of seed its own body . . ." (I Corinthians 15:36–38).

A seed dies, is placed in the earth, then blossoms forth into a stalk, and then produces the grain. The dying is the process by which it takes on the new form. But the seed never loses its identity, for a wheat kernel always produces a wheat stalk, and a corn seed always produces a corn stalk. A rose produces roses.

So it is with human death, says Paul. ". . . not all flesh is alike, but there is one kind for men, another for animals, another for birds, and another for fish. There are celestial bodies and there are terrestrial bodies . . . . If there is a physical body, there is also a spiritual body" (I Corinthians 15:39, 40, 44).

As the farmer prepares the soil, plants, waters, watches the seeds grow from roots, to stalks, to blossoms, and finally rejoices on the day of harvest; so God must rejoice in the great harvest of mature, Christlike men and women. This is the purpose of His creation. The earth is the soil for the roots which shall grow and blossom into a heavenly harvest. Who, then, can doubt the Psalmist's assertion: "Precious in the sight of the Lord, is the death of his saints"?

VINDICATION AT LAST

(For a Lawyer)

This service is a memorial to one of this area's most distinguished lawyers, _____.

Laws are made for the orderly maintenance of community life, the protection of individuals and groups against oppressive powers, and to safeguard the rights of life, liberty, and the pursuit of happiness. A complex society needs regulations to maintain order. Measures are needed to restrain the aggressive self-will of man, and to assure peaceful coexistence. This is true on national, state, county, and city levels.

We are greatly indebted to those who invest their lives to defend the right and who use their influence and knowledge to build just laws for all men. The one to whom we pay tribute served faithfully and honorably. *He* was respected for *his* integrity, thorough preparation, spirit of fairness, and passion for justice.

His colleagues respected *his* leadership so much that they have written the following resolution, which speaks for itself of their esteem:

The members of the County Bar Association, having assembled on the _____ day of _____, for the purpose of taking such action as is deemed appropriate in honor of our deceased professional *brother*, _____, do hereby adopt the following resolution, to wit:

WHEREAS, death has invaded the ranks of the County Bar Association and removed from our midst one of our most distinguished members in the person of _____, and

WHEREAS, *he* has been a practicing attorney at this Bar for many years, during which time *he* has commanded the friendship and respect of the members of this Bar who have been associated with *him*, and

WHEREAS, *he* had a professional career which will be a lasting memorial to *his* memory,

NOW, THEREFORE, as a token of our esteem for *him* and as a tribute to *his* memory and as an expression of our deepest sympathy for *his* family, we take this means of expression of our sense of loss in *his* death and our desire to pay tribute to the memory of a *man* who has for so long a time been an honored member of our profession.

We commend him to God's keeping.

One of the most beautiful picture windows I have ever seen decorates the rear of a sanctuary wall. It is called "The Gethsemane Window," and it contains, in modern rendition, the symbols of the greatest miscarriage of justice the world has ever known. This cosmic crime has shaken the moral universe. Our Lord was denied a defendant; evil men gloated in pride as they crushed the life from Him. Symbolizing the tragedy, sorrow, and suffering, a cross bisects the window. However, at the top of the cross is the victorious crown of life. Death could not hold Him. The justice of the universe rebelled against such treatment. The power of God prevailed in the end. Life overcame death, love overcame hate, and justice triumphed over evil.

All who involve themselves in the struggle for righteousness, and who take up the Spirit and purposes of Jesus Christ, will find vindication. Beneath the cross is the Father's heart, and His power brings life out of death, victory out of tragedy, and light out of darkness.

THOUGHTS IN THE NIGHT

(For a Military Youth)

Have you ever driven through the mountains on a stormy, foreboding, rainy night? Perhaps heavy, dark clouds hung low, giving a lonely, frightening feeling. Your vision was limited until you came to a clearing where the clouds seemed to lift. Then, here and there, you could see "stars shining in the night." Darkness is always more bearable if you look up at the stars, rather than concentrate on the blackness.

Today, you sit in the shadow of a black night of sorrow and grief, yet in the light of the greatest Hope the world has ever known. There are some thoughts that shine out like stars in the midnight sky. If you concentrate upon them instead of the darkness, they will give you comfort.

First, express gratitude for this boy's life, rather than resentment at his death. It has been a genuine privilege of loving, knowing, and sharing the life of _____. Let us be thankful for those years, rather than submit to the temptation to become bitter.

Hannah, the mother of Samuel, said at the boy's birth, "For this child I prayed, and the Lord hath granted me my petition which I asked of him." What joy he brought to his mother. Since this tragic incident, she has reminisced, as she should, of the precious happenings they have shared as mother and son. Memories flood the mind.

Grace Coolidge, wife of the former President, wrote of her own, similar feelings:

> You, my son,
> Have shown me God.
> Your kiss upon my cheek
> Has made me feel the gentle touch
> Of him who leads us on.

68

This young man's wife shared his life through unforgettable years of marriage. What a joy and satisfaction and oneness of spirit! How much finer and richer in spirit you are! As the poet has said, "It is better to have loved and lost than never to have loved at all."

Throughout this community, where he was reared, is felt the unanimous sense of profound loss. His life was not lived in vain. His influence was for good, and for Christ; his ambition and quality of spirit have profoundly affected multitudes.

> We live in deeds, not years, in thought, not breaths;
> In feelings, not in figures on a dial.
> We should count time by heart throbs. He most lives,
> Who thinks most, feels the noblest, acts the best.[6]

A second star that pierces the darkness: Exercise faith in God's love and wisdom, rather than doubt.

Job, the Old Testament character of tremendous stability and integrity, suffered loss of loved ones, physical malady, and personal tragedy. However, in spite of it all and through all the temptations of doubt, he kept faith in God's love.

Not everything that happens in this world is God's intentional will. It is not God's intended will that any of these perish, but that all live a happy, abundant, and eternal life. God placed us, His children, in an unfinished world, with natural laws that require understanding and proper handling to be used. The law of gravity is necessary for man to live on this planet; if it is stretched or disregarded or not properly utilized, it can cause disaster. Man was created free, in order to develop into a mature personality. But the accompanying sin and abuse of man has caused greed, injustice, and war. The human race has a struggle to overcome war. War is man's making, not God's intention. In such circumstances, it becomes God's circumstantial will that men strive for peace, restrain evil tyrants, and build brotherhood. In the processes, some men, such as this one, lose their lives.

All life is so intertwined. We share the guilt of injustice and wars. There is a human element. We share also the riches and liabilities of human progress. Just as when a football team strives for victory and some of the players are injured, so as the human family seeks brotherhood, many persons suffer for the sake of the whole.

A final star to see: Be hopeful of the future, rather than despairing.

The crucifixion and resurrection teach two things: first, that the most innocent of the world do not escape death; and second, there is a Power to surmount even this tragedy. "Death" is not the final word —"resurrection" is. God is alive and has the last word. Jesus said,

69

"Because I live, you shall also live." This is the hope that sustains. Resurrection means that consciousness and recognition go on—even if beyond our ability to comprehend.

Do not grieve for them like the rest of men who have no hope. What is beyond this life is more beautiful, more meaningful, more real than what we now have. "Eye hath not seen, ear hath not heard. . . ." God is the *Alpha* and the *Omega*. He prepared and provided for us here on earth; how much more He provides for us in the future life. "Thanks be unto God who gives us the victory through our Lord Jesus Christ." If we have God, then we are not separated from those who love Him and have gone on to be with God.

An Episcopal clergyman, the Reverend Ernest D. Vandenburgh, wrote a letter of instructions for his survivors, in which he said: "I don't want you to visit my grave. I have no intention of ever being anywhere near it after my funeral, so I do not see why you should be. I hope to have more interesting things to do than to worry over my ashes or dust, and I expect you to, also."

> Let them in, Peter, they are very tired;
> Give them the couches where the angels sleep.
> Let them wake whole again to new dawns fired
> With sun, not war. And may their peace be deep.
> Remember where the broken bodies lie . . .
> And give them things they like. Let them make noise.
> God knows how young they were to have to die! . . .
> Let them love, Peter,—they have had no time—
> Girls sweet as meadow wind, with flowering hair . . .
> They should have trees and bird song, hills to climb—
> The taste of summer in a ripened pear.
> Tell them how they are missed. Say not to fear;
> It's going to be all right with us down here.[7]

A WORKMAN UNASHAMED

(For an Honest Worker)

This is a service in memory of a Christian co-worker who was both an inspiration and a challenge. Through the tears of grief because of our separation, shines the joy of assurance.

The following text contains the basic motivations and principles that directed *his* life. It was the Apostle Paul's admonition to Timothy, his son in the faith, and is relevant to all of us. The Goodspeed translation of II Timothy 2:15 reads: "Do your best to win God's approval as a workman who has nothing to be ashamed of, but rightly shapes the message of truth."

_____ kept that advice close to *his* thoughts, and *he* did *his* best in all three of these things.

First, *he* was a workman who had nothing to be ashamed of. "Take my shiftless influence and bury it with me," said one who came to the end of his days, ashamed of his record. Not so with _____. Aren't you of the family proud of that?

He believed that "honest toil is holy service," that work has sacred significance.

Also, *he* did *his* best to rightly shape the message of truth. There are unnumbered ways to interpret truth. The most effective interpreters are Christian laymen. A teacher can shape the truth by her patience and love for the children at her feet; a clerk, by his unfailing courtesy and cheerfulness; a stenographer, by her accuracy and efficiency; a businessman, by his honesty.

_____ practiced *his* religion. *He* read the New Testament each evening. *He* was a fine steward of *his* earthly possessions, tithing *his* income to the Lord's work. Unnumbered persons, especially college youth, have been encouraged and materially assisted by *his* generosity and personal concern. As the *father* of _____ children, he has been a faithful, wise, and kind family *man*. Through numerous civic and service organizations, *he* let "*his* light shine."

Kathleen Bless, editor of the London *Christian News Letter,* once wrote: "Faith will be strengthened when religion speaks again, not only through the voice of the clerics . . . but through the . . . laymen of all kinds, for whom religion is always indirectly mediated through their life's work." Religion was mediated through the life work, spirit, temper, integrity, and dedication of _____.

However, the basic motive of this *man* was to win God's approval. *He* sought more than the praise of men or the satisfaction of conscience. "What does the Lord require of me?" was *his* basic consideration, and *he* did *his* best to win God's approval. The meaningful times of *his* life were centered in the church. At the time of death, no other approval counts. Only God's approbation has significance!

Hebrews 6:10—". . . God is not unrighteous to forget your work and labour of love . . ." (KJV).

Revelation 14:13—"Blessed are the dead which die in the Lord . . . their works do follow them" (KJV).

I Corinthians 3:14—"If any man's work abide . . . he shall receive a reward" (KJV).

71

Death is the gateway to a world of rewards. This was Paul's advice to Timothy. It is _____'s advice to you, *his* children, and all *his* friends:

First, to take pride in being a workman who has nothing to be ashamed of. In a time when people appear intent upon doing as little as possible, to want pay without production, wages without work, this is good counsel.

Secondly,

> To shape by your living what is true!
> You write a gospel, a chapter a day
> By the deeds that you do, and the words that you say,
> And people judge that gospel whether faulty or true.
> Say—what's the gospel according to you?[8]

Thirdly, and finally, to win God's approval, thus to have that inheritance, incorruptible, and undefiled, reserved in heaven for all of God's children. Hear the Master's welcome: "Well done, good and faithful servant—enter into the joy of the Lord." May we all honor *his* memory by heeding the example and advice of *his* life.

THE BELOVED PHYSICIAN

(For a Physician)

In Colossians 4:14 is recorded the epitaph of a Christian doctor in the first century. It reads: "Luke, the Beloved Physician." He was much loved because it was he who accompanied Paul on his last missionary journey, caring for the Apostle's frail body and sustaining his strength for the Herculean labors by which the seeds of the Gospel were planted in the soil of many nations. Physically, Paul was not a well man. He had a "thorn in his flesh," apparently meaning a physical ailment. He was repeatedly stoned and abused, as were other members of the missionary party. Luke had his hands full, but what a marvelous service he rendered God by keeping the servants well.

We honor today the service of another "beloved physician." Think of all the people whom he has served, from the highest to the humblest, keeping them strong or restoring their health for the tasks of life.

To be a physician takes great spiritual powers of sympathy, tenderness for people, an alert mind, a passion for curing ailments, a responsiveness to incessant calls at all hours of day and night, and bravery in the face of disease and epidemic. Of Jesus it was said: "He saved others; Himself he could not save." But, as one community leader once said, "I'd rather live a little shorter life and be of some service to the world, than to live a long life and do no good."

Many years ago, John Greenleaf Whittier wrote a poem entitled, "The Healer." He sent the poem along with Doré's picture of Christ healing the sick to a young physician friend of his.

It also expresses our appreciation for this physician's work and service to all who have known pain, sickness, and suffering.

> So stood of old the holy Christ
>   Amidst the suffering throng;
> With whom His lightest touch sufficed
>   To make the weakest strong.
>
> That healing gift He lends to them
>   Who use it in His Name;
> The power that filled His garment's hem
>   Is evermore the same.
>
> The paths of pain are thine. Go forth
>   With patience, trust, and hope;
> The sufferings of a sin-sick earth
>   Shall give thee ample scope.
>
> Beside the unveiled mysteries
>   Of life and death go stand,
> With guarded lips and reverent eyes
>   And pure of heart and hand.
>
> So shalt thou be with power endued
>   From Him who went about
> Thy Syrian hillsides doing good,
>   And casting demons out.
>
> That Good Physician liveth yet
>   Thy friend and guide to be;
> The Healer by Gennesaret
>   Shall walk the rounds with thee.[9]

THE LENGTHENED SHADOW OF A MAN'S LIFE

(For a Civic Leader)

The other evening while the sun was going down, I was walking with my back to the west and I noted what a long shadow one's body casts at sundown.

As the sun goes down, we see the lengthened shadow of this *man's* life, and are reminded of the quotation from Proverbs 10:7: "The memory of the just is blessed" (KJV). Indeed it is.

As I have reflected upon the achievements and character and deeds of _____, I have become aware of the extent of *his* unconscious influence. The shadow *he* has cast is of a hard-working, honest, *respected businessman.* From a humble beginning, *his* business has grown to a broad reputation throughout the area. This business is a monument to *his* industry, dependable service, honest dealings, and satisfied customers. "The memory of the just is blessed. . . . Their works do follow them."

The shadow *he* cast is also of a *political and civic leader,* devoted to building a better nation and a wholesome community that is economically sound and culturally literate, with fine schools, parks, and churches. *He* has served many civic positions. "And God is not unrighteous to forget your work and labor of love."

The shadow *he* cast is that of a *devoted churchman and faithful Christian. He* was highly respected by this congregation, and has served the Lord through many years. It is fitting that the family has encouraged friends to donate to the church which was so close to *his* heart. The words of the twenty-third Psalm surely are appropriate: "Surely goodness and mercy shall follow me all the days of my life: and I will dwell in the house of the Lord for ever" (KJV).

The shadow *he* cast is also that of a *devoted family man.* In each of *his* children's homes is a family altar, an influence of their parents. Henrik Ibsen, the Norwegian composer of the House of Rosmersholm, tells about a rector who was tempted to evil. However, he was restrained by the portraits of his godly relatives, which were hanging on the walls of his home. Truly, the memory of this *father* should be an inspiration, challenge, and restraining influence to all of the children of this family.

In II Kings 2:9 is recorded the interesting conversation of Elijah, shortly before his departure from the earth, with his young son in the faith, Elisha. The elderly prophet says: "Ask what I shall do for you, before I am taken from you." The young man, with insight, high ideals, and a profound appreciation, responded, asking not for worldly inheritance, nor fame, nor honor, but rather: "I pray you, let me inherit a double share of your spirit." How fitting a request for children to ask of their parents.

We are saddened by the passing of this great *man,* but in no sense are we defeated, because we believe in God, the resurrection, and the reunion of those who loved *him.*

Longfellow wrote lines about Charles Sumner which make an appropriate conclusion to our tribute:

> Were a star quenched on high,
> For ages would its light,
> Still traveling downward from the sky,
> Shine on our mortal sight.
>
> And so when a great man dies,
> For years beyond our ken
> The light he leaves behind him lies
> Upon the paths of men.[10]

GOD'S HALL OF FAME

(For a Community Servant)

Every five years, names of outstanding Americans are listed in America's Hall of Fame. Only Americans who have been dead for fifty years are eligible for consideration. The definition of success which is used is this: "Fame is durable, good renowned, earned by servants, approved by the wise, applauded by the common people." America still honors her servants as her greatest citizens. Even as Jesus taught long ago, "He who is greatest among you shall be servant of all."

In Hebrews 11 we read of men and women who compose a part of God's Hall of Fame. We who knew this fine *lady* would commend *her* to God for consideration among the great company of famous servants.

_____ is remembered among us as a servant. *She* was active in so many areas of life. I want to share with you the testimony of persons in the organizations in which *she* was so very active. Words always come difficult in paying tribute or giving an estimate of another.

Her employer said of *her*: "*She* was a wonderful friend, and an outstanding employee from every viewpoint in performance and loyalty. You can buy people's time," he said, "but you can't buy their loyalty and dependability. If we wanted something done, *she* would do it. *She* knew how to get a job done, *she* knew everybody, *she* manifested superb leadership, *she* always was doing things for other people. In fact, *she* always thought of doing what most of us think we should have done after an event is over. *She* thought both of the big and the little things."

A spokesman for the Business and Professional *Women's* Chapter said of *her*: "*She* has been the guiding light of this organization through the years. *She* had the unique faculty of being a strong leader *herself,* but *she* also inspired others to lead. *She* was highly respected. All *her* co-workers loved *her*. *She* was one of religious conviction, clean habits, good morals, an influence for good with all who came in contact with *her*. *She* had a deep concern for human beings, a deep compassion. *Her* spirit will be a guiding force for years to come. One couldn't know *her* without feeling that he was a better person for having known *her*."

The Chamber of Commerce passed a resolution expressing their love and appreciation for *her* service to this community in so many ways.

Such service is never in vain. Indeed, *she* has left *her* mark on the sands of time. We would all join our voices in commending *her* for consideration in God's Hall of Fame. "Well done, good and faithful servant. Enter into the joy of our Lord."

THE ARTIST IN RESIDENCE

(For an Artist)

We have come this day to honor the memory of _____. Such a person of diverse talent and interests and with a remarkable quality of character is remembered by different people for different contributions. A daughter and son will express gratitude today for *her mother-liness*; relatives will remember *her* generosity; *her* neighbors and closest friends will remember a warm personality. But perhaps the contribution of which the university, church, and community know *her* best is *her* art work.

It takes a peculiar type of person to become a professional artist— one who has perception, a depth of spiritual quality, an emotional sensitivity, and a determination and skill to reproduce and to communicate.

Frederic Watts, the poet-painter of England, once said concerning his work: "My intention has been not to paint pictures that will charm the eye, as to suggest great thoughts that will appeal to the imagination and kindle all that is best and noblest in humanity. I want to teach people how to live, how to use all their powers, to work and hope and enjoy life, and to care for something higher than money making and selfish pleasure."

Art was also the means by which _____ communicated and revealed *her* deeper feelings and revealed *her* soul. Only a person of emotional maturity could be a successful artist in conveying spiritual truth. Mr. Bailey, an authority on art, once said, "Art is the incarnation of God's beauty." It is a kind of language, communicating through color, form, and line, a depth of truth.

An artist called in a friend to be the first to see his unfinished picture while it stood on the easel. It was a landscape, a view from the studio window. The artist eagerly awaited comment. Finally, the friend said, reprovingly, "Where do you see all those things you put in the picture? Those shadows, those colors? I don't see them out there." The artist looked at his friend in surprise, then answered, "But don't you wish you could?"

A summer missionary to a drab riverside community stepped to the door of an old store which she was trying to make attractive for vacation church school. Burning sunset colors cut her eye, and she stood there motionless. A little girl who had been helping her for the afternoon, came and stood by her for several minutes. "What are you looking at, Teacher?" she asked. "The sunset, Maria; isn't it beautiful?" After a pause, a small voice asked, "May I run home to tell my mother to look?" "I think your mother knows that there is a sunset, Maria." "No she doesn't. She has never thought to look up at it. We don't know it is so beautiful at home." Here we are, a lot of us millionaires in beauty, and some are too hard-pressed to look for beauty. We have eyes that do not see, ears that do not hear. The poet, Cortlandt W. Sayres, has put it this way:

> One midnight deep in starlight still,
> I dreamed that I received this bill—
>   in account with life:
> 5,000 breathless dawns all new;
> 5,000 flowers, fresh and dew;
> 5,000 sunsets, wrapped in gold;
> 1,000,000 snowflakes served ice cold;
> 5 quiet friends, one baby's love;
> 1 white mad sea with clouds above;
> 100 music haunted dreams, moon-drenched
>   roads and hurrying streams;
> A prophesying wind, and trees;
> A silent star and browsing bees;
> One June night in the fragrant woods;
> One heart that loved and understood.
> I wondered when I waked that day,
> How—How in God's name—I could pay.[11]

This is why _____ found in art *her* greatest satisfaction. *She* worked hours on end, day in and day out. Wherever *she* traveled, *she* took lessons in painting. *She* was interested in the masters. *Her* favorite subject to paint was little children. *She* found *her* greatest satisfaction in making people happy through *her* paintings. And though this world never completely satisfies our hunger or our thirst or our deeper needs, yet we do find them satisfied in the next world. I firmly believe that we begin the existence beyond this earth with the spiritual qualities with which we end this one. Kipling explains it beautifully in his poem "L'Envoi":

> When Earth's last picture is painted,
>   And the tubes are twisted and dried,
> When the oldest colors have faded,
>   And the youngest critic has died,
> We shall rest, and, faith, we shall need it—
>   Lie down for an aeon or two,
> Till the Master of All Good Workmen
>   Shall put us to work anew.
>
> And those that were good shall be happy:
>   They shall sit in a golden chair;
> They shall splash at a ten-league canvas
>   With brushes of comets' hair;
> They shall find real saints to draw from—
>   Magdalene, Peter, and Paul;
> They shall work for an age at a sitting,
>   And never be tired at all!
>
> And only the Master shall praise us,
>   And only the Master shall blame;
> And no one shall work for money,
>   And no one shall work for fame;
> But each for the joy of the working,
>   And each, in his separate star,
> Shall draw the Thing as he sees It
>   For the God of Things as They Are![12]

"As we have borne the image of the earthy, we shall also bear the image of the heavenly."

MORE THAN CONQUERORS

(For One Handicapped)

We have come to pay our tribute to the life of _____. We would express our admiration for *his* accomplishments and philosophy

78

of life in spite of being hampered by a bruised and crippled body. Those of us in the counseling field are always impressed by an exemplary person who accepts *his* handicaps without resentment and as an opportunity from God. *He* served society in a way persons who are not handicapped cannot serve. When I first called upon *him*, it was not I who helped *him* as much as *he* who helped me. I went away lifted in spirit with a greater appreciation and a profound humility. *He* loved God, *he* loved life, and *he* loved the church. *He* was not afraid of death.

"Who shall separate us from the love of Christ? shall tribulation, or distress, or persecution, or famine, or nakedness, or peril, or sword? . . . Nay, in all these things we are more than conquerors through him that loved us" (Romans 8:35, 37, KJV).

God does not give us assurance against handicaps, accidents, and trouble. The purpose of Christianity is not the avoidance of difficulties or pain; rather, it produces character and strength adequate to meet hardship when it comes.

The cross of Christ makes two facts plain: first, in this world, even the innocent are not exempt from suffering; secondly, there is a Power able to surmount evil, to rise above tragedy, and to comfort in the face of death. In the cross, we can see God suffering with us; we can see an example of triumph over agony. God puts love in us so that we love others; He puts forgiveness in our spirits so we are not bitter; He gives us an example of how to meet suffering, and how to triumph over death.

"In the world you have tribulation. Be of good cheer. I have overcome the world."

AS THE YEARS ROLL ONWARD

I learn as the years roll onward
    And leave the past behind,
That much I have counted sorrow
    Proves that the world is kind.
That many a flower I long for
    Had a hidden thorn of pain,
And many a rugged bypath led to
    The fields of ripened grain.

The clouds must cover the sunshine,
    They cannot banish the sun
And the earth shines out the brighter
    When the weary rain is done.

We stand in the deepest sorrow
    To see the clearest light
And often from wrong's own darkness
    Comes the very strength of right.

So, the heart from the hardest trial
    Gains the purest joy of all
And from lips that have tasted sadness
    The sweetest songs will fall.
For as peace comes after suffering
    And love is rewarded pain
So after death comes heaven
    And out of our loss the gain.[13]

THE BATON IS YOURS

(For an Athlete)

The author of the Hebrew letter apparently had been a frequent witness of the ancient Olympic races. In the 11th chapter, he pictures life as a relay race we run. He gives us a glimpse of those who have run the race before us, the great forerunners of his nation who had followed God—Abraham, Joseph, Moses, and others. He ends the chapter by declaring: "And all these, though well attested by their faith, did not receive what was promised, since God had foreseen something better for us, that apart from us they should not be made perfect." He goes on to admonish: "Therefore, since we are surrounded by so great a cloud of witnesses, let us also lay aside every weight, and sin which clings so closely, and let us run with perseverance the race that is set before us, looking to Jesus the pioneer and perfecter of our faith . . ." (Hebrews 12:1, 2).

Life is much like a relay race, and we all are the middlemen. No one starts from scratch. Others have run the course before us, and we start at the point where their lives touch ours. Our parents came down the track; for awhile we run along beside them, until they are able to pass the baton of their work and character and faith on to us; then our parents slow down and eventually step out of the race, while we carry on the responsibility. Ultimately, we come to the time when we transfer our interests and unfulfilled hopes and faith on to our children and community. Thus, life is linked to life, generation to generation, and on and on goes the race.

We are humbled with a sense of indebtedness. Paul the Apostle felt this way: "I am debtor both to the Greeks and Barbarians, the wise and the unwise." The human family could be divided roughly into two groups: those who feel they are giving more than they get, and those who feel they are getting more than they give. All of us have received more than we deserve. As Chesterton wrote: "He who is conscious of a debt he can never pay, will be forever paying it."

That fact also sobers us with a sense of responsibility. A recently bereaved mother, planning for the security of her home following her husband's death, said to her oldest boy, "Son, you must take over where your father left off." We see today the unfinished tasks left behind which we are compelled to carry on. It is our responsibility to pass on the baton of our faith and spiritual heritage.

Walk through a cemetery and read the stones: "Born 1920—Died 1942"; "Born 1930—Died 1951"; "Born 1940—Died 1965." War snuffed out the lives of many young men before their tasks were completed. We carry on where they left off in preserving freedom, democracy, and liberty of conscience.

Another young Man died at the age of thirty-three in the midst of establishing the Kingdom of God on earth. We must carry on His dream and work of redemption, lest the world forget, lest the victory be lost.

THE MESSENGER OF THE LORD

(For a Minister of the Gospel)

Were we to turn to the eulogies of men today, what eloquent appraisals of our brother we could hear. Person after person who has been blessed by his effective, Godly ministry could speak at length. The churches he has served, the fellow pastors with whom he has associated, the denominational leaders with whom he labored, all could write endless epitaphs to his memory. Nevertheless, we turn to the Lord's evaluation in Malachi 2:5–7 regarding another messenger of another era; the words are fitting to this dear pastor: ". . . says the Lord of hosts. My covenant with him was a covenant of life and peace, and I gave them to him, that he might fear; and he feared me, he stood in awe of my name. True instruction was in his mouth, and no wrong was found on his lips. He walked with me in peace and uprightness, and he turned many from iniquity. For the lips of a priest should guard knowledge, and men should seek instruction from his mouth, for he is the messenger of the Lord of hosts."

His was a career of Christian witness characterized by patience, love, sacrifice, dedication, concern, discipline, scholarship, faithfulness, unselfishness. Like Abraham, he went where he was called, and was faithful in all things. Like Moses, he led the people of God from

81

doubts and fears to confidence in the face of difficulties. Like Joshua, he loved his country and fought and suffered for its success. Like Jonathan, he met many a discouraged brother and cheered him by giving him the strength from God. Like David, he sang the church to victory and shouted on the battle of triumph. Like Isaiah, he constantly pointed the church to brighter days and better things in the future. Like Daniel, he was true through life to the teaching of his boyhood. Like Malachi, he believed in bringing all the tithes into the Lord's storehouse. Like John the Baptist, he delighted to preach to multitudes, "Behold the Lamb of God who taketh away the sins of the world." Like St. John, he believed with all his soul that Jesus was the Son of God. Like Peter, he honored Christ by being an instrument of the Holy Spirit. Like Paul, he rejoiced that Jesus died for all men, and he did his best to let the world know this blessed truth with pen and sermon. He pled for the church to send the gospel to all. Like Jesus, his Divine Master, whom he daily followed, "he went about doing good." Like Enoch, "he walked with God and he was not, for God took him."[14]

He was a consecrated Christian and minister, true to his God, his country, his church, his wife, his family, and his fellowmen. The world is richer because he lived, served, and died in the faith.

> Servant of God, well done.
>   Rest from thy loved employ;
> The battle fought, the victory won,
>   Enter Thy Master's joy.
>
> The pains of death are past,
>   Labor and sorrow cease,
> And life's long warfare closed at last,
>   Thy soul is found in peace.
>
> Servant of God, well done.
>   Thy glorious warfare past;
> The battle's fought, the race is won
>   And thou art crowned at last.[15]

A SCIENTIST'S VIEW OF IMMORTALITY

(For a Scientist)

Today we honor the contributions of a scientist who has been involved in the physical progress of man. He has helped probe the far reaches of space; he has helped release the amazing power of the atom—both unbelievable achievements. It is significant to note, however, that this man was also a man of God; operating from a Christian context, and dedicated to spiritual principles. He knew, as all great scientists know, that whether atomic energy, space travel, or science proves to be an earthly blessing or the source of her destruction, is dependent upon spiritual and moral directions. He was a man of faith, believing in the essentially unknowable—that which cannot be absolutely proven. The scientific method is to build a reasonable hypothesis, based upon experience, observation, and progmatic verification. From this hypothesis, the scientist proceeds with a leap of faith.

Two chief premises about life this man assumed: one is belief that every person has to account for what he does with God's gift of life on earth. The other is belief that man has an immortal soul, which will cherish the reward or suffer the penalty decreed in that judgment.

Many people in our modern world feel that scientists have outgrown such ideas, but many scientists have a real surprise for the skeptics. Science, for example, tells us that nothing in nature, not even the tiniest particle, can disappear without a trace. Think about that for a moment. Once you do, your thoughts about life will never be the same. Science has found that nothing can disappear without a trace. Nature does not know extinction; all it knows is transformation. Benjamin Franklin, a scientist, put it well: "I believe . . . that the soul of man is immortal and will be treated with justice in another life respecting its conduct in this."

Now, if God applies this fundamental principle to the most minute and insignificant parts of His universe, does it not make sense to assume that He applies it also to the masterpiece of His creation—the human soul? I think it does. As Dr. Wernher von Braun has said so well, "Everything science has taught me and continues to teach me strengthens my belief in the continuity of our spiritual existence after death. Nothing disappears without a trace." May this man's faith give us encouragement and strength.

VI.

Biblical Meditations

MORE STATELY MANSIONS

Paul the Apostle, who had tremendous insight into the mysteries of life and death, said, "There is a natural body, and there is a spiritual body" (I Corinthians 15:44, KJV).

Death is the transition from one body to another.

A person unfamiliar with the workings of nature would be hard put to find much beauty in a caterpillar. Yet, that caterpillar ultimately lays aside its cocoon and turns into a gorgeous, multicolored butterfly. This is a part of God's marvelous design and the God-given forces of nature.

THE BUTTERFLY

I hold you at last in my hand,
    Exquisite child of the air.
Can I ever understand
    How you grew to be so fair?

. . . .

Now I hold you fast in my hand,
    You marvelous butterfly,
Till you help me to understand
    The eternal mystery.

From that creeping thing in the dust
    To this shining bliss in the blue!
God give me courage to trust
    I can break my chrysalis too![1]
           —*Alice Freeman Palmer*

God gives us humans earthly bodies for the first phase of our lives just as He gives us our first baby teeth. When the baby teeth are no longer useful, they come out and second teeth come in. It may be a painful process. Just so, our earthly bodies are useful for a while, and then they are replaced by "spiritual," or "glorified," bodies.

Paul says that the difference between a natural body and a spiritual body is somewhat like the difference in the seed, the stalk, and the flower of a plant. The life of the plant lives first in the seed, then in another body—the stalk, and finally in a third kind of body—the flower. ". . . unless a grain of wheat falls into the earth and dies, it remains alone; but if it dies, it bears much fruit" (John 12:24).

We live for a time in our natural bodies, until they grow too old or get too sick for us to live in them any longer. Then, through a dying process, we are remarkably transformed into a beautiful, recognizable, spiritual body.

One of the truly inspiring, famous American poems conveys this imagery of life's progressive development. It is entitled "The Chambered Nautilus," by Oliver Wendell Holmes. The poet, who loved the sea, examined the shell of a pearly nautilus. The shell was a spiral of gradually enlarging compartments in which a mollusk, likened to the snail, successively lived as it grew larger and larger. As the little creature that lived inside the shell outgrew one chamber, it moved on to the next, where it could grow and develop further, then on to a still larger chamber, until it was finally free, leaving its shell behind. Dr. Holmes was fascinated by the analogy to the human soul and spirit, which must continually move on, expand, grow, and stretch, building ever more stately mansions.

> Build thee more stately mansions, O my soul,
>> As the swift seasons roll!
>> Leave thy low-vaulted past!
> Let each new temple, nobler than the last,
> Shut thee from heaven with a dome more vast,
>> Till thou at length art free,
> Leaving thine outgrown shell by life's unresting sea![2]

THE LOVE OF GOD
Psalm 23

If we were to select the most favored section of Scripture, the passage which lies closest to the hearts of men and which springs most readily to their lips, it probably would be the twenty-third Psalm. It has given comfort, strength, and hope to those in sorrow in all generations because its poetic images describe the character and activity of God.

"The Lord is my shepherd." In the early morning the ancient shep-

herd's custom was to lead the sheep to green grass and pure water. During the day he would protect the sheep from wild animals and minister to their hurts and bruises. At the close of day the shepherd would bring the sheep into the shelter and safety of a fold. Gradually, the sheep subconsciously felt that as long as they had this shepherd, all their needs would be met. It is the picture of a sleepless, far-sighted, weather-beaten shepherd looking over his scattered sheep, every one of them on his heart. His staff is a symbol of guidance; his rod is a symbol of defense. He does not drive his sheep, but leads them in the Eastern manner. His wisdom, goodness, and concern for their welfare are beyond the comprehension of his flock.

The image is so real that it is not surprising in the crises of life that man has turned to this Psalm to be assured of God's love. "The Lord is my shepherd."

Probably this Psalm was written by David at an old age, as he looked back to see how God had satisfied his needs.

The following phrases indicate what God does for us:

"He makes me lie down." In Him is rest, peace, and quiet refuge.

"He leads me." He gives guidance and a sense of direction.

"He restores my soul." In Him is renewal, revival, and reinvigoration.

"He is with me." He offers His companionship, a sense of His presence. We are never alone.

"He prepares a table for me." He is the Host offering hospitality to His chosen guests.

"He annoints my head with oil." He gives His blessings with abundant generosity, beyond deserving, until *"My cup overflows."*

Dr. Charles L. Allen testifies to his trust in God. On his study desk is a paperweight, a glass globe filled with water; inside there is a man. Every now and then, Dr. Allen will get upset, pick up the paperweight, and shake it. When shaken, the globe gets all cloudy and snowy inside. Then he begins to talk to the little man inside: "Little man, I know you are disturbed. You are being shaken up, and your world is being shaken up; it's all cloudy, and you can't see. You don't know what might happen, and you're afraid. Little man, I want to assure you I have you right here in my hand, and I have your world right here in my hand, and I am strong enough to hold it." Then he holds it still, and the cloudiness clears up and the snowy flakes settle down. Then he says, "You see, little man, you didn't have anything to worry about at all."

The Bible says, "In God's hands are the deep places of the earth. The strength of the hills is His also." "He's got the whole world in

His hands . . . you and me, brother . . ." is the refrain of a popular spiritual. But God is a great God, wise and eternal, tender and loving. He is our Heavenly Father.

Therefore, do not fear, even though you walk through the valleys and the shadows. The shadows are like fog that hides the light for a moment; soon they vanish, and the light will shine. There could be no shadows without the light in the first place.

Since God is like a shepherd, you need not want. What more do you need than what He has given and promised? Out of His great love, He has planned and provided for your needs here and in the hereafter. Do not worry; only trust Him. He will not forsake you.

Surely, your response to His love is to dwell in the house of the Lord forever, to remain in His fellowship throughout life and eternity, and to claim His forgiveness and communion.

The story is told of the celebrated actor who one night attended a party given in his honor. During the course of the evening, the guests requested that he give some recitations of various literary pieces. Finally a request was made for him to recite the twenty-third Psalm. As he did so, his timing, inflections, and diction were perfect. His voice was deep and confident. It was a great display of oratory; and he sat down in the midst of a loud applause. Then someone asked the elderly pastor, a friend of the actor since his youth, who had been invited, if he would recite the same Psalm. He was hesitant, but the actor insisted. So the gray and bent pastor began. His voice wavered and was husky. His diction was not sharp. But when he spoke, he emphasized the personal pronouns: "The Lord is _my_ shepherd, _I_ shall not want. . . ." The room grew still. When he finished, there was no applause, only reverent stillness. Eyes were damp with tears. It had been a spiritual experience. Presently the silence was broken by the actor, who said in subdued tones, "My friends, I know the twenty-third Psalm; our pastor friend knows the Shepherd."

It is not the Psalm, but the Shepherd, that comforts and consoles.

BEYOND WITH THE MASTER

John Baillie, writing on the nature of eternal life, tells of a dying patient who asked his doctor if he could tell him anything about what lay ahead. While the doctor was fumbling for a reply, he heard a scratching at the door, and it gave him his answer: "Do you hear that?" he asked. "That is my dog. I left him downstairs, but he grew impatient, has come up, and hears my voice. He has no notion what is inside the door, but he knows I am here. Now, is it not the same with you? You do not know what lies beyond the door, but you know your Master is there."

Jesus did not give detailed descriptions of eternal life, but He did say, ". . . I go to prepare a place for you . . . that where I am you may be also" (John 14:2, 3). One can assume that heaven is the kind of realm wherein Christ would feel at home. It is not a strange, fearsome place, because Jesus is there.

Since Jesus showed His love for the beautiful things on earth, we can believe that there will be beauty yonder, the loveliness of the simple and the genuine, such as He said surpassed Solomon in all his glory. (Luke 12:27).

Since Christ was a Great Teacher, who said, ". . . you will know the truth, and the truth will make you free" (John 8:32), we can expect heaven to be a school, where we shall learn the truth about ourselves, the meaning of mysterious misfortunes and tragedies, and where we shall know others even as we are known—not for our reputation, but for our character, and not for our wealth, but for our worth.

Along with beauty and truth will be the other ultimate value—goodness. Not the pale, anemic piety which is often mistaken for real goodness, but the virtue of integrity and love which is creative and challenging.

Eternal life is the extension of what we have developed here on earth. If we have not learned to like what Christ liked, then we shall not be comfortable in the place He has prepared for us. But if we have learned to live with the true, the beautiful, and the good, and to love what Christ loved, then death shall be the door to where Christ is.

The Promise that Consoles

It is said that when one of his flock was dying, John Watson, the Scottish preacher of Edinburgh, would kneel down and whisper in the ear, "In my Father's house are many rooms." Then, with a contented sigh, they would "slip away" entirely unafraid. There is something about this great portion of Scripture which consoles.

"Let not your hearts be troubled"—because there is a faith that dispels fear.

When it seemed to the disciples that everything was shaking, collapsing, and coming to an end, when they were disquieted by the certainty of Jesus' death, He told them not to worry, not to be alarmed, nor be afraid.

He said, *"believe in God."* Believe that there is God, and that you

88

are not alone. You are not left to manage for yourself, because God is the Beginning and the End, the One "from everlasting to everlasting." Underneath are His everlasting arms. He was before all things, and He will endure beyond all things. You do not need to despair if He is the Object of your faith.

Then Jesus added, *"believe also in me."* It is good to believe in God, but such belief needs to be focused and made clear. Jesus was the Revelation of what the character of God is like. A little boy who had been injured in an auto accident was terrified. On the way to the hospital, he wailed, "I am going to die and go to God and I'm scared." "Don't you love God?" his mother asked. "I hate Him!" the child cried. The wise mother said, "When you die, you go where Jesus is." With that the child was comforted. He loved Jesus. Jesus makes God personal, near, and lovable. Jesus, who wept with compassion over the lonely, was revealing a God of tender love. Jesus, who conquered the grave, was revealing a God who has power even over death. "I am the Way, the Truth, and the Life. . . . No man cometh unto the Father but by me." A faith in God as seen in Jesus Christ will dispel your fears about death.

"In my Father's house are many mansions . . ." is the promise that brings hope. This is a beautiful picture of God's spacious creation. It is a home; there is a Father there. Home represents everything that is good, precious, and splendid. It is a fortress of love, a sanctuary of happiness. This earth, with its green meadows, shining stars, and steadfast hills, is one room. Heaven, with its unknown, unseen, and eternal beauty, is another room. There is life to be lived with the Father here, and there is life to be lived with the Father there. Death is the passing from one room to another. Dying might mean pain and loneliness to those left behind; but the torment and sorrow is lessened by the realization that it is a triumph.

". . . if it were not so, would I have told you . . ." is the basis of our assurance. We can depend upon the promise because we can depend upon Jesus. Everything He stood for, has been right and true. He founded the highest system of ethics the world has ever known. We can rely upon that. His promises never fail. This is assured knowledge.

"I go to prepare a place for you. . . ." Christ has prepared the way; He has gone on ahead. When a loved guest is coming to our home, preparations are made which are designed to meet his tastes and needs. Jesus has arranged a place for each of us, according to our particular needs.

God wants all of His family to gather home. Today, we feel like a friend of Dr. Drummond's felt when he said, "The home going of Drummond adds one more incentive to Heaven"; and like John White Chadwick felt when he sang:

> More homelike seems the vast unknown,
> Since they have entered there;
> To follow them were not so hard,
> Wherever they may fare;
> They can't be where God is not,
> On any sea or shore;
> What e'er betides, thy love abides,
> Our God, forever more.[3]

"I will come again and take you to myself, that where I am you may be also."

Dr. E. Wilson, who was part of an Antarctic crew that perished, wrote this to his wife, who was left behind:

Don't be unhappy. We are playing a good part in a great scheme arranged by God himself, and all is well. We will all meet after death, and death has no terrors. All is for the best to those that love God, and we have both loved Him with all our lives. Life itself is a small thing to me now, but my love for you is for ever and a part of our love for God. All the things I had hoped to do with you after this expedition are as nothing now, but there are greater things for us to do in the world to come. All is well.

GOD'S AMAZING KNOWLEDGE

Jesus, the Supreme Revealer of God, taught that no detail in the entire universe escapes the Heavenly Father's knowledge. To His doubting disciples He spoke words assuring them that God cared for each one as though he were the only one to care for.

Said Jesus, "Are not two sparrows sold for a penny? And not one of them will fall to the ground without your Father's will . . . Fear not, therefore; you are of more value than many sparrows" (Matthew 10:29, 31). Think of what Jesus was saying! There are literally billions of birds in the world; there are 500 different species of hummingbirds alone. These, in contrast to man, are of little worth. Yet, said Jesus, God knows even when one falls to the ground. How much more does He know you; and how much more is He concerned about you.

If God cares for anything on this earth, it must be for people. The Psalmist asked, "When I consider the heavens, the work of thy fingers, the moon and the stars which thou ordained, what is man that thou art mindful of him? Thou hast made him a little lower than the angels." If God knows when a sparrow falls to the earth, how much more does He know man's name and circumstances. Man is the supreme object of God's creation. We are children of His, made in His "spiritual image," with the abilities of thought, memories, dreams, and self-transcendence. God loves you and your loved ones.

The mathematical immensity of the human race is great, to be sure. There are over two and one-half billion people on this planet, with three new generations each century, and the centuries reach back beyond historic record. To say that God is concerned and knows each person by name seems ridiculous. One is tempted to think that no one could distinguish between the concerns of each; however, consider your own experience in knowing people. When you were a child, perhaps there were only a dozen people in your tiny world—your mother, father, brother, and a few playmates. Beyond that, your immature mind could not go. By the time you were in grade school, you became acquainted with forty or fifty distinct individuals. And the number increased every year. By the time you reached your twenties, perhaps there were several hundred whom you knew personally. Perhaps you now know several thousand. The greater the mind, the less confusing the massive numbers. If this is the capacity of the finite human mind, that has developed only a few years, relatively speaking, what then must be the capacity of the infinite mind of God?

In the famous Sermon on the Mount, the Master Teacher said, ". . . what man of you, if his son asks him for bread, will give him a stone? Or if he asks for a fish, will give him a serpent? If you then, who are evil, know how to give good gifts to your children, how much more will your Father who is in heaven give good things to those who ask him!" (Matthew 7:9–11). We are concerned and provide for our own. How much more does God provide for His own, even beyond the span of earthly years.

9/14/77

CONFIDENCE THAT REMAINS UNSHAKEN

Rom. 8:35–39

"Who shall separate us from the love of Christ?" (ROMANS 8:35)

To be separated, or alienated, from God's love is the most regretful state possible. Such a condition would leave one helpless and forlorn.

Is there anything that can so pull us apart from Him? Paul lists some of the most frequently recurring and powerful adversaries to the human life, evils which confront human beings in their extremities: tribulations, distress, persecutions, famine, nakedness, peril, sword, the physical hardships, mental anguish, unjust treatment.

91

As powerful and interfering and disruptive as these can be, Paul says they cannot change God's attitude toward us. True, we may become embittered and resentful—*our* attitudes toward God may change; but *His* attitude toward us never changes.

"No," says Paul, "we are more than conquerors *through Him who loved us. . . .*" Think of it! What a superlative victory! The evil we confront cannot separate us from God's love because of the spiritual vitality caused by His love. Our victory is through Him who loved us.

We are not necessarily delivered from misfortunes, pain, or even a cross. As it is written, "For thy sake we are being killed all the day long; we are regarded as sheep to be slaughtered" (Romans 8:36).

We are not delivered by the gospel from misfortune or death, yet in all of this one is able to find a blessing. Our sorrow becomes the expositor of mysteries unexplained.

Our tragedies become the sources of our deepest understanding. We can not only defeat the powers of evil, but also snatch a blessing from our tragedies. The sorrows which blight our joys become the sources of our deepest growth. The powers which sting us are transformed into positive influences.

Paul the Apostle said, ". . . I am persuaded, that neither death, nor life, nor angels, nor principalities, nor powers, nor things present, nor things to come, nor height, nor depth, nor any other creature, shall be able to separate us from the love of God, which is in Christ Jesus our Lord" (Romans 8:38, 39, KJV). Nothing which threatens the oblivion of what God holds dear can overthrow the good which He intends for us.

So long as we remain loyal to Christ, there is nothing in this life or the life to come that can defeat us. Even the haunting fears of the mystery and finality of death are allayed. No dimension of space and no passage of time can affect our confidence. God's love depends upon no circumstances, nor chronology. Our security rests on none of the things in which we are tempted to place our confidence.

Rather, ". . . thanks be to God, who gives us the victory through our Lord Jesus Christ. Therefore, my beloved brethren, be steadfast, immovable, always abounding in the work of the Lord, knowing that in the Lord your labor is not in vain" (I Corinthians 15:57, 58).

AND THEN THE DAWN

In the New Testament, when Jesus announced the death of the brother of Martha and Mary, He said, "Our friend Lazarus has fallen asleep . . ." (John 11:11). "Sleep" is one of the suggestive Scriptural metaphors of "death." When Stephen was stoned, the account reads,

"He fell asleep." The deceased at Thessalonica, Paul says, were "those who are asleep" (I Thessalonians 4:13). When the early Christians referred to a burial ground, they used the word *coemeterium*, which was the same in both Greek and Latin. From it our English word "cemetery" comes, which literally means "a sleeping chamber."

Death in a sense is like sleep because it brings rest. Can anyone think of anything more desirable or delicious than to lie down and sleep when weary after a hard day's work? It is rest from labor.

One of the reasons why heaven was pictured as a place of rest to the ancient peoples is that they were burdened with manual labor and were always tired, and a heaven of sleep had great appeal. Jesus pitched His invitations to the oppressed, saying, "Come to me all you who labor and are heavy laden, and I will give you rest." Many people die in their sleep, and others pass through a merciful coma, which eases the path from consciousness to death. When our bodies are worn out and can no longer serve us, we simply lie down to sleep.

However, picturing death as "sleep" indicates an awakening in the morning. Jesus said to Mary and Martha about their brother, "I go, that I may awake him out of sleep." Refreshed by rest, one picks up the thread of life and goes on again. We go to sleep, only to wake up again. First comes the night, and then the dawn.

Within the memory of most of us is when, as children, our mother or father tucked us in bed, spoke a word of assurance or prayer, and then gave us a good-night kiss. We went to sleep contented, confident that we would be refreshed when awakened on the tomorrow. What is more, we knew we would find our father's or mother's love continuing just where the good-night kiss left off.

> So I looked up to God,
> And while I held my breath
> I saw Him slowly nod,
> And knew—as I had never known ought else,
> With certainty sublime and passionate
> Shot through and through
> With sheer unutterable bliss—
> I knew
> There was no death but this,
> God's kiss,
> And then the waking to an Everlasting Love.[4]
> —*G. A. Studdert Kennedy*

Peter Marshall, the chaplain of the United States Senate during the demanding years following World War II, suffered a heart attack at the age of forty-two. As he was being taken from his home to the hospital by ambulance, he kissed his wife and son, then said confidently, "I'll see you in the morning." Those were his last words to them, because he died before seeing his family again. Nevertheless, he articulated our faith. We do believe that "in the morning" we will see one another.

Do not mourn. "I'll see you again in the morning."

THROUGH THE SHADOWS

"Yea, though I walk through the valley of the shadow of death, I will fear no evil . . ." (Psalm 23).

Phillips Brooks, one of the greatest ministers to grace an American church pulpit, called this the "nightingale of the Psalms" because the nightingale sings its sweetest when the night is the darkest. I have a feeling that for most of us the darkest night is when someone that we love more than we love ourselves slips out of this life into the next, or when we ourselves are facing death.

Surely this is what David was illustrating. In Palestine there actually was a valley named the Shadow of Death. It was a frightening place for the sheep to go through. But David, in picturing this crisis experience, was saying in essence, "Don't lose your head; remember that you're not alone." Underscore the word *through*: "Yea, though I walk *through*. . . ." You can stand anything, if you know you are going to get *through*.

There are four things to remember about the shadows:

They hide and distort reality. In the valley of death, the pathway may look dark and gloomy. The shadows may hide the beauty and give the impression that there is no safety or security ahead. But faith causes us to know that the way ahead is safe, secure, and beautiful. When you pass *through*, a new day will banish the shadows and you will see, face to face, the reality of that which lies before.

A second thing to remember is that the *shadows themselves have no reality*. There is nothing to fear or dread in a shadow. It may hide reality, but the shadow is not real. It does not change anything. Whenever there is a shadow, we have positive proof that there is light shining beyond. There can be no shadow without light. The shadow is nothing but the resultant gloom caused by something between you and the light.

Too, *shadows vanish when you face the light*. When you walk toward the light, you never see a shadow; it is only when you turn your back to the light that the shadows are before you.

When you turn to look where you have been, and relive the past,

94

the shadows deepen and the gloom of death increases. Turn and look into the life ahead; the light of the Eternal shines in your face, and the shadows are no more.

Finally, the *shadows that seem so dreadful and fearful really bring out the glory and beauty of life.*

Have you ever watched an artist paint a landscape? He will brush in the sky, then paint the ground, putting in the trees, the grass, and the other objects. He will paint them in all their detail. Every line, every object, stands out in clear relief. You marvel at the careful detail of it, and you feel that here is a master of nature. You believe the picture to be complete and ready for framing. But just when you think it is perfect, the artist begins to put in the shadows. With wide brush strokes, he covers the carefully painted detail with dark, drab shadows. The beautiful details which he labored so hard to perfect seem to be covered with ugly, dark shadows. You cry out, "You have ruined the picture with those dark shadows!"

With saddened heart you walk away, but from a distance you look back with utter amazement. The shadows which you thought had spoiled the painting have brought out its beauty. The painting has now become a masterpiece. The shadows have made the picture beautiful. At close range the shadows seem to spoil it all; but viewed from a distance, a better perspective and appreciation are possible.

Life is like that. The dark shadows, which we fear and dread, are really the touch of the Artist that makes of our lives masterpieces of beauty, worthy to be hung in the gallery of the Eternal forever.

THE RIVER OF LIFE

"Then he showed me the river of the water of life, bright as crystal, flowing from the throne of God and of the Lamb through the middle of the street of the city; also, on either side of the river, the tree of life with its twelve kinds of fruit, yielding its fruit each month; and the leaves of the tree were for the healing of the nations. There shall no more be anything accursed, but the throne of God and of the Lamb shall be in it, and his servants shall worship him; they shall see his face, and his name shall be on their foreheads. And night shall be no more; they need no light of lamp or sun, for the Lord God will be their light, and they shall reign forever and ever" (Revelation 22:1–5).

"There is a river whose streams make glad the city of God, the holy habitation of the Most High" (Psalm 46:4).

"Time" is the passing of events from the not yet, through the now, to the no more.

Tennyson likened "life" to a "river": "Time like an ever-rolling stream bears all its sons away."

At a conference on the banks of the Black River, near Carlsbad Caverns, New Mexico, this analogy came alive to me.

The Black River appears mysteriously out of the barren, dry earth, originating from hidden and eternal sources. Underneath the surface are the springs which give it birth. So is the beginning of our life. Down deep is the "ground of our being." Mysterious is our beginning and appearance on earth. We have come from the bosom of the eternal love and plan of the Heavenly Father.

The rather narrow stream of the Black River, presently, however, is fed by other streams that originate on the earth's surface. Some are muddy waters traveling over miles of the watershed. Some are drainage from overflow irrigation streams. Still others are the sewage release from the camps along its shores.

How like our life, that is fed by many sources and influenced by many streams of thought and activity, some of which color or may even pollute the purity of our lives.

At the waterfalls, a communion table was set up on the banks of the Black River. From that vantage point the stream passed over rocks, where it moved rapidly, dancing in the sunlight, throwing spray about, and gushing over the intermittent falls. Here the impurities were removed from the water, the course was concentrated, and sounds roared and sung as the water moved into a large, peaceful pool.

In every life, a person meets crises of obstacles he must handle, rough places he must move over, barriers he must go around, and falls he must endure. Often it comes in youth; at other times in young adulthood.

At such a crisis, how often we come to encounter Jesus Christ and the cross at our side. In such a moment, life becomes deeper; we concentrate our purposes; we make our commitment; we are purified and cleansed through shaking experience; then we plunge into the stream of His will. There we find peace, depth, usefulness, and joy.

The large pool in the Black River has fish living there; large trees bend their branches over it; green grass grows beside it; birds wing happily about it. In its calm, placid movement, it reflects the beauty of the earth; and in the moonlight, the majesty of heaven.

So our life, when in fellowship with Christ, is beautiful and useful. We give encouragement to our surroundings, build large the tree of God's Kingdom, and reflect the glory of His Being.

Soon, however, the pool of the Black River narrows; the banks essentially squeeze it in. Then it moves only a little way, around a bend, where it is not seen; ultimately the river mysteriously disappears, back into the earth.

To all comes the time when sickness hems us in, narrows our circulation, and makes a turn that puts us out of sight. Life moves haltingly along, until death mysteriously takes us back into the deep from whence we came.

However, the amazing thing about the Black River is that twenty miles or so down the line, the river reappears.

Death is not the end. The promise to those who love God is that they shall live again! It has been verified by the resurrection of Jesus, our Lord.

This is the river "whose streams make glad the city of God, the holy habitation of the Most High" (Psalm 46:4).

THE VICTORY OVER DEATH

The fifteenth chapter of I Corinthians is a Christian declaration of faith in immortality and a definition of the basis of that faith. It is not exactly an argument, but it does state the reasons for believing in life everlasting, and it gives some of the implications of such a belief. It uses the analogies of nature and human experience to make clearer what death means and why life conquers death. The basic assertion is, "Death is swallowed up in victory" (I Corinthians 15:54).

There are three approaches to immortality: first, reason says that it may be so; secondly, conscience says that it ought to be so; thirdly, Christianity says that it is so.

The best that reason can do for us is to assure us that immortality is in the realm of possibility. No amount of argument can really convince. You can search in vain in existing philosophies for the final word. The scientific method, or the logical approach, cannot prove the reality of the future realm. This does not mean that the philosophical approach should be discarded, but it does mean that reason cannot give us the assurance we crave.

Actually, religious belief ought to be able to stand any reasonable test. We do not believe what is contrary to experience or reason. Though the Christian faith cannot be proven, this does not mean that faith is blind; nonetheless, it is faith, not proof. However, some of the greatest minds of all time have grappled with the problem, and they have come to the belief that immortality may be so.

On a deeper level, conscience says that immortality ought to be so. You cannot live very seriously without becoming aware of the inconsistencies of life that is confined to this earth. A man soon gets troubled at the shortness of human life and the inadequacy of his few years. An inner voice objects to human personality being extinguished.

In Thornton Wilder's *The Bridge of San Luis Rey,* a pestilence visits Brother Juniper's village. Brother Juniper draws up a chart of the characteristics of fifteen victims and fifteen survivors, rating them for such qualities as goodness, piety, usefulness. When he adds up the total for the victims and compares them with that for the survivors, his figures show that the dead were five times more worth saving than those who lived through the pestilence. This unexpected result causes Brother Juniper great distress of mind, and it does for many of us as well.

The terrible inequities of human life on earth are a good reason for believing in immortality. Justice demands that the rights be rewarded and the wrongs be punished, if not on earth, then in the future world. This moral argument becomes ever more pressing when we find ourselves unable to accept the idea of extinction. The better our lives become, the more insistent is the idea that immortality ought to be so.

Finally, Christianity says that immortality is so in a way that is utterly convincing. Men cannot walk with Christ without having their doubts fly away. We appeal to the historical account of a Person called Jesus, who walked this earth, was killed, and yet by the power of God was raised. This great historical testimony has been the keystone of our faith. Here we enter a realm deeper than logic and more positive than conscience. It is not guesswork; it is certainty. We trust the character, teachings, and Person of Jesus, who said, "If it were not so, I would have told you."

FROM SUNSET TO SUNRISE

Easter is a festival of the dawn! Clement of Alexandria, one of the early church fathers, caught the significance of Easter when he wrote: "Christ has turned our sunsets into sunrise." In the resurrection narrative itself, the record says, "They came unto the sepulchre at the rising of the sun," and life was never the same again.

At sunset, it seemed that the universe did not care what happened to its righteous; at sunrise, the disciples knew that at its heart was an Invincible Power, that it was designed by benevolent intelligence, tempered by limitless love, directed by holy purpose.

At sunset, the cross seemed a horrible implement of execution from which everyone cringed; at sunrise, it became a reverent and holy symbol, before which the world kneels in adoration and rises with inspiration.

At sunset, the grave, sealed with an immovable boulder and heavily guarded, seemed conclusive evidence that death was the end; with the coming of dawn, however, was the proof that man has forever, and outlives death; the grave represents an expectant adventure into life eternal. "O death, where is thy sting? O grave, where is thy victory?"

At sunset, only minor chords of hopeless existence were heard; at sunrise, the exuberant harmonies of joyous and meaningful living were sung.

At sunset, a Galilean rabbi, Jesus of Nazareth, was dead; at sunrise, He was truly the Christ of God, the risen Lord of Glory.

At sunset, the obscure disciples were a timid, discouraged, disillusioned, weary lot; at sunrise, they were transformed, confident, courageous crusaders who went forth to defy kings, to proclaim Christ, and to change the world.

Easter was the day that changed the world. Easter is the festival of the dawn. If you can catch the spirit, power, and significance of this day, it can turn your sunsets into sunrise.

The Easter dawn should turn your questions into renewed certainty of life's invisibles. Thomas, the hard-headed logician, was the typical materialist among the disciples. His faith, like the others, had dwindled completely when Jesus died. When it was announced that Jesus had risen and was alive, he replied, "Except I see, I will not believe." Then the risen Lord appeared, and Thomas, falling down, cried, "My Lord, my God." Jesus said, "Because you have seen me, you believe; blessed are they who have not seen me but who believe."

". . . he hath given assurance unto all men, in that he hath raised him from the dead" (ACTS 17:31 KJV).

VII.

Funeral Music

There need not be music at every funeral. The minister should always ask the family if they would like it or not. Frequently, there may be only organ music. When vocal music is wanted, it is not the wisest to use "favorite hymns" of the deceased. Rather, the minister should have the privilege of choosing music that will complement his theme, be spiritually upbuilding, and provide the appropriate mood. He should counsel with the family about his recommended selections. It is the author's opinion that in no other aspect of the modern funeral is there greater need for reform—too much of the funeral music has been melancholy and sad, whereas it should be triumphant and faith-building, focusing upon the joys of the "New Jerusalem." The music should be about life and the greatness of God, rather than "death's cold sullen stream" or "going down the valley one by one." Congregational singing is used increasingly, enabling family and friends to participate in the release of emotion and the affirmation of faith; almost unanimously the bereaved have testified to its helpfulness. Following is a list (in no sense exhaustive) of meaningful suggestions.

ORGAN PRELUDES AND POSTLUDES

Bach—Hark, a Voice Saith, All Is Mortal
    O God, Have Mercy
    Our Father, Thou Art in Heaven Above
    Our Father, Who Art in Heaven
Brahms—Deck Thyself, My Soul
    A Lovely Rose Is Blooming
    O Sacred Head Now Wounded
    O World, I Now Must Leave Thee
Dupré—He, Remembering His Great Mercy
Franck—Andanta *from* Grande Pièce Symphonique
Greenfield—Prelude in Olden Style
Guilmant—Funeral March and Song of the Seraphs
    Prayer and Cradle Song

Karg-Elert—Adorn Thyself, O My Soul
  O God, Thou Faithful God
  Rejoice Greatly, O My Soul
Mendelssohn—Adagio *from* The First Organ Sonata
Muffat—Adagio *from* Toccata
Purvis—Communion

Appropriate Hymns

(For Congregational, Choral, or Solo Singing)

For First Part of Service

Angel Voices, Ever Singing (*for a child*)
Come, Thou Fount of Every Blessing
Come, Ye Disconsolate
Great Is Thy Faithfulness
Hark! Hark, My Soul! Angelic Songs (*evening*)
My Faith Looks Up to Thee
Now Thank We All Our God
Our God, Our Help in Ages Past
Unto the Hills Around Do I Lift Up ("Sandon")
What a Friend We Have in Jesus

For Middle of Service

Beneath the Cross of Jesus
Brief Life Is Here Our Portion
Come, O Thou Traveler Unknown
Dear Lord and Father of Mankind
How Firm a Foundation, Ye Saints of the Lord
I Heard the Voice of Jesus Say
In the Hour of Trial
Jesus, Lover of My Soul
Love Divine, All Loves Excelling
O Christ, the Way, the Truth, the Life
O God of Bethel, by Whose Hand
O Love that Wilt Not Let Me Go
O Master, Let Me Walk with Thee
Savior, Like a Shepherd Lead Us (*for a child*)
The King of Love My Shepherd Is
The Lord's My Shepherd, I'll Not Want
There is a Green Hill Far Away
When I Survey the Wondrous Cross ("Hamburg")

For Conclusion of Service

Around the Throne of God in Heaven (*for a child*)
Crown Him with Many Crowns
For All the Saints Who from Their Labors Rest
Guide Me, O Thou Great Jehovah
Jerusalem the Golden
Lead, Kindly Light ("Sandon")
Now the Laborer's Task Is O'er
One Sweetly Solemn Thought
O Jesus, I Have Promised
O Mother Dear, Jesusalem
O What Their Joy and Their Glory Must Be (*O Quanta Qualia*)
Sunset and Evening Star
Ten Thousand Times Ten Thousand

SOLOS AND DUETS

Christiansen—I Know a Home Eternal (*baritone*)
Franck—O Lord Most Holy
Gaul—They Shall Hunger No More (*soprano and alto*)
Gounod—Forever with the Lord (*duet, high and low*)
Handel—Come unto Him (*soprano*)
    He Shall Feed His Flock (*alto*)
    I Know that My Redeemer Liveth
        (*all from* The Messiah)
Handel-Milligan—Immortal Love (*high*)
Harker—How Beautiful the Mountains
Kingsley—Immortality
Knapp-Crosby—Open the Gates of the Temple
MacDermid—In My Father's House
Shelley—Hark, Hark, My Soul
Ward-Stephens—In My Father's House
Willeby—Crossing the Bar (*duet, high and low*)

CHORAL ANTHEMS

Bach—Now Let Every Tongue Adore Thee
    Ah, How Fleeting
Barnby—Crossing the Bar
Barnby-Lewis—Now the Day Is Over (*men's voices*)
Chadwick—When Our Heads Are Bowed with Woe

Gaul—Great and Marvelous (The Holy City)
    No Shadows Yonder (The Holy City)
Gounod—Forever with the Lord (*quartet*)
    Unfold, Ye Portals Everlasting (Redemption)
Grieg—Jesu, Friend of Sinners
Haydn—Lo, My Shepherd Is Divine
Matthews—I Heard a Voice from Heaven
Mendelssohn—Forever Blest Are They (*men's voices*)
    Happy and Blest Are They
    He that Shall Endure to the End
Noble—The Souls of the Righteous
Parker—The Lord Is My Light
Spohr—Blest Are the Departed
Shelley—Crossing the Bar (*solo, low voice, with chorus*)
Stainer—God So Loved the World
    My Hope Is in the Everlasting
Tschaikowsky-Cain—O Blest Are They

VIII.

Funeral Service Materials

OPENING SENTENCES

"The eternal God is your dwelling place, and underneath are the everlasting arms" (Deuteronomy 33:27a).

" 'It is the Lord who goes before you; he will be with you, he will not fail you or forsake you; do not fear or be dismayed' " (Deuteronomy 31:8).

"Our soul waits for the Lord; he is our help and shield" (Psalm 33:20).

" 'Seek the Lord while he may be found, call upon him while he is near . . .' " (Isaiah 55:6).

"Come to me, all who labor and are heavy laden, and I will give you rest' " (Matthew 11:28).

". . . they who wait for the Lord shall renew their strength, they shall mount up with wings like eagles, they shall run and not be weary, they shall walk and not faint" (Isaiah 40:31).

" 'Be still, and know that I am God' " (Psalm 46:10a).

"Cast your burden on the Lord, and he will sustain you . . ." (Psalm 55:22a).

"Let us . . . with confidence draw near to the throne of grace, that we may receive mercy and find grace to help in time of need" (Hebrews 4:16).

". . . the Lord is a refuge to his people, a stronghold to the people of Israel" (Joel 3:16b). "For thou, O Lord, art my hope, my trust . . ." (Psalm 71:5).

"Our help is in the name of the Lord, who made heaven and earth" (Psalm 124:8). "To thee, O Lord, I lift up my soul" (Psalm 25:1a).

104

"We know that in everything God works for good with those
love him" (Romans 8:28a).

"The Lord is my light and my salvation; whom shall I fear?
Lord is the stronghold of my life; of whom shall I be afraid?" (Ps
27:1).

"For God alone my soul waits in silence; from him comes my salv
tion. He only is my rock and my salvation . . ." (Psalm 62:1–2a)

". . . fear not, for I am with you, be not dismayed, for I am your
God; I will strengthen you, I will help you, I will uphold you with
my victorious right hand. . . . For I, the Lord your God, hold your
right hand; it is I who say to you, 'Fear not, I will help you' " (Isaiah
41:10, 13).

"When you pass through the waters I will be with you; and through
the rivers, they shall not overwhelm you; when you walk through fire
you shall not be burned, and the flame shall not consume you" (Isaiah
43:2).

"For as heavens are high above the earth, So great is his lovingkind-
ness toward them that fear him. . . . Like as a father pitieth his children, so Jehovah pitieth them that fear him" (Psalm 103:11, 13 ASV).

INVOCATIONS

Eternal God, who lovest us with an everlasting love: help us now
to wait upon Thee with reverent and submissive hearts, that as we *may*
hear the words of eternal life, we may through the comfort of the
Scriptures have hope in Jesus Christ, and be lifted above our darkness
and distress into the light and peace of Thy presence, through Jesus
Christ, our Lord. Amen.

O Christ of God, through whom we look beyond the veil of flesh
and blood, who art a Window into the reality of God, by whom we
have come to believe that our most lasting values lie in the spirit, and
in fellowship with whom we have realized a kinship with our Heavenly
Father: quiet us with confidence, strengthen us with faith, and inspire
us with hope for the tomorrows, through Jesus Christ. Amen.

Gracious God, whose mercies are new with every morning, on a
wintry day we seek the springtime of Thy presence; in the midst of
years that melt like snowflakes, we would rest in Thine everlastingness;
as no wind makes the flame of the sun to falter, and no storm disturbs
the stars, so steadfast is Thy love. Thou art the Home of our souls,

105

and our lives are cold, wintry, and lonely without Thee. By Thy grace and companionship, save us from darkness, despair, and loneliness, through Jesus Christ. Amen.

Eternal Spirit, who out of the mysterious womb of nature has created us, with minds to see truth, hearts to love beauty, and wills to serve Thee: hush us before the glory of Thy greatness, sober us with knowledge of the insecurity of our lives, cause us to number our days and to live responsibly before Thee, in whose hands is the future and our only hope, through Jesus Christ. Amen.

All-Powerful God, who turned the cross into a resurrection, and the darkness of death into a morning of light and new life: we thank Thee for the glow of faith and hope that rises in our hearts this day, through the knowledge of Jesus Christ, our Lord, who verified that love is stronger than hate, that life outlasts death, and who said, "Because I live, you shall live also." Amen.

Holy, Transcendent God, yet intimate and personal, nearer than hands and feet, known in Jesus Christ, our Lord: we pray to Thee. Thou art the Artist of colors and places unknown to us; Thou art the Lord of Stars beyond our sight, yet Thou hast come to us, in sandals, to show the Way, the Truth, and the Life. In Thee is our trust; in the trust is our comfort; and in the comfort is our peace, through Jesus Christ, our Lord. Amen.

O Infinite Source of Life, Truth, and Joy: Thou art the Light of every heart that sees Thee, the Life of every soul that loves Thee, the Strength of every mind that seeks Thee: from our narrow world, we would enter into Thy greater world, and from our temporal view we would move into Thy larger view, and from this temporal life we would take hold of eternal life, with Jesus Christ as our Leader and Lord. Amen.

SCRIPTURE READINGS

Our Christian faith is made for times such as this. The Scriptures speak to our most acute personal needs with a wisdom that has been built upon the experience of untold generations who met the tribulations of life and became "more than conquerors." Listen to their testimonies of faith, and you will find renewed hope.

Glorious Assurance

"The Lord is my shepherd, I shall not want. . . . Even though I walk through the valley of the shadow of death, I fear no evil; for thou

art with me; thy rod and thy staff, they comfort me" (Psalm 23:1, 4).
"For this perishable nature must put on the imperishable, and this
mortal nature must put on immortality. When the perishable puts on
the imperishable, and the mortal puts on immortality, then shall come
to pass the saying that is written: 'Death is swallowed up in victory' "
(I Corinthians 15:53, 54). ". . . neither death, nor life, nor angels,
nor principalities, nor things present, nor things to come, nor powers,
nor height, nor depth, nor anything else in all creation, will be able to
separate us from the love of God in Christ Jesus our Lord" (Romans
8:38, 39). " 'Let not your hearts be troubled; believe in God, believe
also in me. In my Father's house are many rooms; if it were not so,
would I have told you that I go to prepare a place for you? And when
I go and prepare a place for you, I will come again and will take you
to myself, that where I am you may be also' " (John 14:1–3). ". . . and
death shall be no more, neither shall there be mourning nor crying
nor pain any more, for the former things have passed away" (Revelation 21:4). " 'They shall hunger no more, neither thirst any more;
the sun shall not strike them, nor any scorching heat. For the Lamb
in the midst of the throne will be their shepherd, and he will guide
them to springs of living water; and God will wipe away every tear
from their eyes' " (Revelation 7:16, 17).

Victory Over Tribulations

"God is our refuge and strength, a very present help in trouble"
(Psalm 46:1). " 'When you pass through the waters I will be with
you; and through the rivers, they shall not overwhelm you; when you
walk through fire you shall not be burned, and the flame shall not
consume you. For I am the Lord your God . . .' " (Isaiah 43:2, 3a).
"He said, 'The Lord is my rock, and my fortress, and my deliverer,
my God, my rock, in whom I take refuge, my shield and the horn
of my salvation, my stronghold and my refuge, my savior . . .' " (II
Samuel 22:2, 3). "What then shall we say to this? If God is for us,
who is against us? He who did not spare his own Son but gave him
up for us all, will he not also give us all things with him? Who shall
bring any charge against God's elect? It is God who justifies; who is
to condemn? Is it Christ Jesus, who died, yes, who was raised from
the dead, who is at the right hand of God, who indeed intercedes for
us? Who shall separate us from the love of Christ? Shall tribulation,
or distress, or persecution, or famine, or nakedness, or peril, or sword?
. . . No, in all these things we are more than conquerors through him
who loved us" (Romans 8:31–35, 37). "For this slight momentary
affliction is preparing for us an eternal weight of glory beyond all

comparison, because we look not to the things that are seen but to the things that are unseen; for the things that are seen are transient, but the things that are unseen are eternal" (II Corinthians 4:17–18).

The Resurrected Life

"But we would not have you ignorant, brethren, concerning those who are asleep, that you may not grieve as others do who have no hope. For since we believe that Jesus died and rose again, even so, through Jesus, God will bring with him those who have fallen asleep" (I Thessalonians 4:13–14). "If for this life only we have hoped in Christ, we are of all men most to be pitied. But in fact Christ has been raised from the dead, the first fruits of those who have fallen asleep" (I Corinthians 15:19, 20). "What is sown is perishable, what is raised is imperishable. It is sown in dishonor, it is raised in glory. It is sown in weakness, it is raised in power. It is sown a physical body, it is raised a spiritual body. If there is a physical body, there is also a spiritual body. Thus it is written, 'The first man Adam became a living being'; the last Adam became a life-giving spirit" (I Corinthians 15:42–45). "Just as we have borne the image of the man of dust, we shall also bear the image of the man of heaven. I tell you this, brethren: flesh and blood cannot inherit the kingdom of God, nor does the perishable inherit the imperishable. Lo! I tell you a mystery. We shall not all sleep, but we shall all be changed, in a moment, in the twinkling of an eye, at the last trumpet. For the trumpet will sound, and the dead will be raised imperishable, and we shall be changed. For this perishable nature must put on the imperishable, and this mortal nature must put on immortality" (I Corinthians 15:49–53). "But thanks be to God, who gives us the victory through our Lord Jesus Christ. Therefore, my beloved brethren, be steadfast, immovable, always abounding in the work of the Lord, knowing that in the Lord your labor is not in vain" (I Corinthians 15:57, 58).

God's Provisions

"The Lord is my light and my salvation; whom shall I fear? The Lord is the stronghold of my life; of whom shall I be afraid?" (Psalm 27:1). "When I am afraid, I put my trust in thee. In God, whose word I praise, in God I trust without a fear. What can flesh do to me?" (Psalm 56:3, 4). ". . . I heard a voice from heaven saying, 'Write this: Blessed are the dead who die in the Lord henceforth.' 'Blessed indeed,' says the Spirit, 'that they may rest from their labors, for their deeds follow them!' " (Revelation 14:13). "But, as it is written, 'What no

108

eye has seen, nor ear heard, nor the heart of man conceived, what God has prepared for those who love him'" (I Corinthians 2:9). "Then the King will say to those at his right hand, 'Come, O blessed of my Father, inherit the kingdom prepared for you from the foundation of the world; for I was hungry and you gave me food, I was thirsty and you gave me drink, I was a stranger and you welcomed me, I was naked and you clothed me, I was sick and you visited me, I was in prison and you came to me.' . . . 'Truly, I say to you, as you did it to one of the least of these my brethren, you did it to me'" (Matthew 25:34–36, 40). "Then I saw a new heaven and a new earth; for the first heaven and the first earth had passed away, and the sea was no more. And I saw the holy city, new Jerusalem, coming down out of heaven from God, prepared as a bride adorned for her husband; and I heard a great voice from the throne saying, 'Behold, the dwelling of God is with men. He will dwell with them, and they shall be his people, and God himself will be with them . . .'" (Revelation 21:1–3). "For we know that if the earthly tent we live in is destroyed, we have a building from God, a house not made with hands, eternal in the heavens" (II Corinthians 5:1).

True Security *assorted scriptures*

"'Do not lay up for yourselves treasures on earth, where moth and rust consume and where thieves break in and steal, but lay up for yourselves treasures in heaven, where neither moth nor rust consumes and where thieves do not break in and steal. For where your treasure is, there will your heart be also'" (Matthew 6:19–21). "'. . . a man's life does not consist in the abundance of his possessions'" (Luke 12:15). "For what will it profit a man, if he gains the whole world and forfeits his life?" (Matthew 16:26). "'Blessed are the poor in spirit, for theirs is the kingdom of heaven. Blessed are those who mourn, for they shall be comforted. Blessed are the meek, for they shall inherit the earth. Blessed are those who hunger and thirst for righteousness, for they shall be satisfied. Blessed are the merciful, for they shall obtain mercy. Blessed are the pure in heart, for they shall see God. Blessed are the peacemakers, for they shall be called sons of God. Blessed are those who are persecuted for righteousness' sake, for theirs is the kingdom of heaven. Blessed are you when men revile you and persecute you and utter all kinds of evil against you falsely on my account. Rejoice and be glad, for your reward is great in heaven, for so men persecuted the prophets who were before you'" (Matthew 5:3–12). "'Every one then who hears these words of mine and does them will be like a wise man who built his house upon the rock; and the rain fell, and the floods came, and the winds blew and beat upon that house, but it did not fall, because it had been founded on the rock. And every one who hears these words of mine and does not do them will be like a foolish man who built his house upon the sand; and the rain fell, and the floods came, and the winds blew and beat against that house, and it fell; and great was the fall of it' " (Matthew 7:24–27).

For a Child

"He will feed his flock like a shepherd, he will gather the lambs in his arms, he will carry them in his bosom . . ." (Isaiah 40:11).

"The Lord is my shepherd, I shall not want; he makes me lie down in green pastures. He leads me beside still waters; he restores my soul. He leads me in paths of righteousness for his name's sake. Even though I walk through the valley of the shadow of death, I fear no evil; for thou art with me; thy rod and thy staff, they comfort me. Thou preparest a table before me in the presence of my enemies; thou anointest my head with oil, my cup overflows. Surely goodness and mercy shall follow me all the days of my life; and I shall dwell in the house of the Lord for ever" (Psalm 23).

"I lift up my eyes to the hills. From whence does my help come? My help comes from the Lord, who made heaven and earth. He will not let your foot be moved, he who keeps you will not slumber. Behold, he who keeps Israel will neither slumber nor sleep. The Lord is your keeper; the Lord is your shade on your right hand. The sun shall not smite you by day, nor the moon by night. The Lord will keep you from all evil; he will keep your life. The Lord will keep your going out and your coming in from this time forth and for evermore" (Psalm 121).

"As a father pities his children, so the Lord pities those who fear him. For he knows our frame; he remembers that we are dust. As for man, his days are like grass; he flourishes like a flower of the field; for the wind passes over it, and it is gone, and its place knows it no more. But the steadfast love of the Lord is from everlasting to everlasting upon those who fear him, and his righteousness to children's children, to those who keep his covenant and remember to do his commandments" (Psalm 103:13–18).

". . . Jesus . . . said to them, 'Let the children come to me, do not hinder them; for to such belongs the kingdom of God. Truly, I say to you, whoever does not receive the kingdom of God like a child shall not enter it.' And he took them in his arms and blessed them, laying his hands upon them" (Mark 10:14–16).

110

"At that time the disciples came to Jesus, saying, 'Who is the greatest in the kingdom of heaven?' And calling to him a child, he put him in the midst of them, and said, 'Truly, I say to you, unless you turn and become like children, you will never enter the kingdom of heaven. Whoever humbles himself like this child, he is the greatest in the kingdom of heaven. Whoever receives one such child in my name receives me. . . . See that you do not despise one of these little ones; for I tell you that in heaven their angels always behold the face of my Father who is in heaven'" (Matthew 18:1–5, 10–11).

For a Youth

"God is our refuge and strength, a very present help in trouble. Therefore we will not fear though the earth should change, though the mountains shake in the heart of the sea; though its waters roar and foam, though the mountains tremble with its tumult" (Psalm 46:1–3).

"When you pass through the waters I will be with you; and through the rivers, they shall not overwhelm you; when you walk through fire you shall not be burned, and the flame shall not consume you" (Isaiah 43:2).

"Who shall separate us from the love of Christ? shall tribulation, or anguish, or persecution, or famine, or nakedness, or peril, or sword? . . . Nay, in all these things we are more than conquerors through him that loved us. For I am persuaded, that neither death, nor life, nor angels, nor principalities, nor things present, nor things to come, nor powers, nor height, nor depth, nor any other creature, shall be able to separate us from the love of God, which is in Christ Jesus our Lord" (Romans 8:35, 37–39, ASV).

" 'Peace I leave with you; my peace I give to you; not as the world gives do I give to you. Let not your hearts be troubled, neither let them be afraid'" (John 14:27).

"Beloved, now are we children of God, and it is not yet made manifest what we shall be. We know that, if he shall be manifested, we shall be like him; for we shall see him even as he is" (I John 3:2, ASV). ". . . now we see in a mirror, darkly; but then face to face: now I know in part; but then shall I know fully even as also I was fully known" (I Corinthians 13:12, ASV).

For the Middle-Aged

"I wait for the Lord, my soul waits, and in his word I hope; my soul waits for the Lord more than watchmen for the morning, more than watchmen for the morning. O Israel, hope in the Lord! For with the Lord there is steadfast love, and with him is plenteous redemption. And he will redeem Israel from all his iniquities" (Psalm 130:5–8).

"Blessed be the God and Father of our Lord Jesus Christ, the Father of mercies and God of all comfort, who comforts us in all our affliction, so that we may be able to comfort those who are in any affliction, with the comfort with which we ourselves are comforted by God" (II Corinthians 1:3–4).

"Therefore, since we are surrounded by so great a cloud of witnesses, let us also lay aside every weight, and sin which clings so closely, and let us run with perseverance the race that is set before us, looking to Jesus the pioneer and perfecter of our faith, who for the joy that was set before him endured the cross, despising the shame, and is seated at the right hand of the throne of God" (Hebrews 12:1–2).

"For all who are led by the Spirit of God are sons of God. . . . it is the Spirit himself bearing witness with our spirit that we are children of God, and if children, then heirs, heirs of God and fellow heirs with Christ, provided we suffer with him in order that we may also be glorified with him. I consider that the sufferings of this present time are not worth comparing with the glory that is to be revealed to us. . . . If God is for us, who is against us? He who did not spare his own Son but gave him up for us all, will he not also give us all things with him? Who shall bring any charge against God's elect? It is God who justifies; who is to condemn? Is it Christ Jesus, who died, yes, who was raised from the dead, who is at the right hand of God, who indeed intercedes for us?" (Romans 8:14, 16–18, 31–34).

"And I heard a voice from heaven saying, 'Write this: Blessed are the dead who die in the Lord henceforth.' 'Blessed indeed,' says the Spirit, 'that they may rest from their labors, for their deeds follow them!' " (Revelation 14:13).

Josh 1:9   _For Persons of Advanced Years_   _Bible – Eccles. 3:1–8_

"The Lord is my light and my salvation; whom shall I fear? The Lord is the stronghold of my life; of whom shall I be afraid? . . . One thing have I asked of the Lord, that will I seek after; that I may dwell in the house of the Lord all the days of my life, to behold the beauty of the Lord, and to inquire in his temple. For he will hide me in his shelter in the day of trouble; he will conceal me under the cover of his tent, he will set me high upon a rock. . . . I will sing and make melody to the Lord. . . . Wait for the Lord; be strong, and let your heart take courage; yea, wait for the Lord!" (Psalm 27:1, 4–5, 6b, 14).

" 'Lord, let me know my end, and what is the measure of my days; let me know how fleeting my life is! Behold, thou hast made my days a few handbreadths, and my lifetime is as nothing in thy sight. . . . And now, Lord, for what do I wait? My hope is in thee. Deliver me from all my transgressions. . . . Hear my prayer, O Lord, and give ear to my cry; hold not thy peace at my tears! For I am thy passing guest, a sojourner, like all my fathers' " (Psalm 39:4–5, 7–8, 12).

"The years of our life are threescore and ten, or even by reason of strength fourscore; yet their span is but toil and trouble; they are soon gone, and we fly away. . . . So teach us to number our days that we may get a heart of wisdom. . . . Let thy work be manifest to thy servants, and thy glorious power to their children. Let the favor of the Lord our God be upon us, and establish thou the work of our hands upon us, yea, the work of our hands establish thou it" (Psalm 90:10, 12, 16, 17).

" 'Behold, happy is the man whom God reproves; therefore despise not the chastening of the Almighty. For he wounds, but he binds up; he smites, but his hands heal. . . . You shall know that your tent is safe, and you shall inspect your fold and miss nothing. You shall know also that your descendants shall be many, and your offspring as the grass of the earth. You shall come to your grave in ripe old age, as a shock of grain comes up to the threshing floor in its season. Lo, this we have searched out; it is true. Hear, and know it for your good' " (Job 5:17–18, 24–27).

"Now faith is the assurance of things hoped for, the conviction of things not seen. For by it the men of old received divine approval. By faith we understand that the world was created by the word of God, so that what is seen was made out of things which do not appear. By faith Abel offered to God a more acceptable sacrifice than Cain, through which he received approval as righteous, God bearing witness by accepting his gifts; he died, but through his faith he is still speaking. By faith Enoch was taken up so that he should not see death; and he was not found, because God had taken him. Now before he was taken he was attested as having pleased God. And without faith it is impossible to please him. For whoever would draw near to God must believe that he exists and that he rewards those who seek him" (Hebrews 11:1–6).

"Jesus said to her, 'I am the resurrection and the life; he who believes in me, though he die, yet shall he live, and whoever lives and believes in me shall never die. Do you believe this?' " (John 11:25–26).

113

"Blessed is the man who walks not in the counsel of the wicked, nor stands in the way of sinners, nor sits in the seat of scoffers; but his delight in the law of the Lord, and on his law he meditates day and night. He is like a tree planted by streams of water, that yields its fruit in its season, and its leaf does not wither. In all that he does, he prospers. The wicked are not so, but are like chaff which the wind drives away. Therefore the wicked will not stand in the judgment, nor sinners in the congregation of the righteous; for the Lord knows the way of the righteous, but the way of the wicked will perish" (Psalm 1).

"O Lord, who shall sojourn in thy tent? Who shall dwell on thy holy hill? He who walks blamelessly, and does what is right, and speaks truth from his heart; who does not slander with his tongue, and does no evil to his friend, nor takes up a reproach against his neighbor; in whose eyes a reprobate is despised, but who honors those who fear the Lord; who swears to his own hurt and does not change; who does not put out his money at interest, and does not take a bribe against the innocent. He who does these things shall never be moved" (Psalm 15).

"A good wife who can find? She is far more precious than jewels. The heart of her husband trusts in her, and he will have no lack of gain. She does him good, and not harm, all the days of her life. . . . She opens her hand to the poor, and reaches out her hands to the needy. . . . Strength and dignity are her clothing. . . . She opens her mouth with wisdom, and the teaching of kindness is on her tongue. She looks well to the ways of her household, and does not eat the bread of idleness. Her children rise up and call her blessed; her husband also, and he praises her: 'Many women have done excellently, but you surpass them all'" (Proverbs 31:10–12, 20, 25a, 26–29).

"Blessed be the God and Father of our Lord Jesus Christ! By his great mercy we have been born anew to a living hope through the resurrection of Jesus Christ from the dead, and to an inheritance which is imperishable, undefiled, and unfading, kept in heaven for you, who by God's power are guarded through faith for a salvation ready to be revealed in the last time. In this you rejoice, though now for a little while you may have to suffer various trials, so that the genuineness of your faith, more precious than gold which though perishable is tested by fire, may redound to praise and glory and honor at the revelation of Jesus Christ. Without having seen him you love him; though you do not now see him you believe in him and rejoice with

114

unutterable and exalted joy. As the outcome of your faith you obtain the salvation of your souls" (I Peter 1:3-9).

Other Appropriate Scriptures

"As a hart longs for flowing streams, so longs my soul for thee, O God. My soul thirsts for God, for the living God. . . . Why are you cast down, O my soul, and why are you disquieted within me? Hope in God; for I shall again praise him, my help and my God" (Psalm 42:1, 2, 11).

"He who dwells in the shelter of the Most High, who abides in the shadow of the Almighty, will say to the Lord, 'My refuge and my fortress; my God, in whom I trust.' For he will deliver you from the snare of the fowler and from the deadly pestilence; he will cover you with his pinions, and under his wings you will find refuge; his faithfulness is a shield and buckler. You will not fear the terror of the night, nor the arrow that flies by day, nor the pestilence that stalks in darkness, nor the destruction that wastes at noonday. . . . Because you have made the Lord your refuge, the Most High your habitation, no evil shall befall you, no scourge come near your tent" (Psalm 91:1-6, 9-10).

" 'For as the Father raises the dead and gives them life, so also the Son gives life to whom he will. The Father judges no one, but has given all judgment to the Son, that all may honor the Son, even as they honor the Father. He who does not honor the Son does not honor the Father who sent him. Truly, truly, I say to you, he who hears my word and believes him who sent me, has eternal life; he does not come into judgment, but has passed from death to life. Truly, truly, I say to you, the hour is coming, and now is, when the dead will hear the voice of the Son of God, and those who hear will live. For as the Father has life in himself, so he has granted the Son also to have life in himself, and has given him authority to execute judgment, because he is the Son of man. Do not marvel at this; for the hour is coming when all who are in the tombs will hear his voice and come forth, those who have done good, to the resurrection of life, and those who have done evil, to the resurrection of judgment' " (John 5:21-29).

"I love the Lord, because he has heard my voice and my supplications. Because he inclined his ear to me, therefore I will call on him as long as I live. The snares of death encompassed me; the pangs of Sheol laid hold on me; I suffered distress and anguish. Then I called on the name of the Lord: 'O Lord, I beseech thee, save my life!' Gracious is the Lord, and righteous; our God is merciful. The Lord preserves the simple; when I was brought low, he saved me. Return, O my soul, to your rest; for the Lord has dealt bountifully with you. For thou hast delivered my soul from death, my eyes from tears, my feet from stumbling. . . . I kept my faith, even when I said, 'I am greatly afflicted'. . . . What shall I render to the Lord for all his bounty to me? I will lift up the cup of salvation and call on the name of the Lord, I will pay my vows to the Lord in the presence of all his people. Precious in the sight of the Lord is the death of his saints" (Psalm 116:1–8, 10, 12–15).

"O Lord, thou hast searched me and known me! Thou knowest when I sit down and when I rise up; thou discernest my thoughts from afar. Thou searchest out my path and my lying down, and art acquainted with all my ways. Even before a word is on my tongue, lo, O Lord, thou knowest it altogether. Thou dost beset me behind and before, and layest thy hand upon me. Such knowledge is too wonderful for me; it is high, I cannot attain it. Whither shall I go from thy Spirit? Or whither shall I flee from thy presence? If I ascend to heaven, thou art there! If I make my bed in Sheol, thou art there! If I take the wings of the morning and dwell in the uttermost parts of the sea, even there thy hand shall lead me, and thy right hand shall hold me. If I say, 'Let only darkness cover me, and the light about me be night,' even the darkness is not dark to thee, the night is bright as the day; for darkness is as light with thee. . . . How precious to me are thy thoughts, O God! How vast is the sum of them! If I would count them, they are more than the sand. When I awake, I am still with thee" (Psalm 139:1–12, 17–18).

"So we do not lose heart. Though our outer nature is wasting away, our inner nature is being renewed every day. For this slight momentary affliction is preparing for us an eternal weight of glory beyond all comparison, because we look not to the things that are seen but to the things that are unseen; for the things that are seen are transient, but the things that are unseen are eternal" (II Corinthians 4:16–18). "For we know that if the earthly tent we live in is destroyed, we have a building from God, a house not made with hands, eternal in the heavens. Here indeed we groan, and long to put on our heavenly dwelling, so that by putting it on we may not be found naked. For while we are still in this tent, we sigh with anxiety; not that we would be unclothed, but that we would be further clothed, so that what is mortal may be swallowed up by life. He who has prepared us for this very thing is God, who has given us the Spirit as a guarantee. So we are always of good courage; we know that while we are at home in the

116

body we are away from the Lord, for we walk by faith, not by sight. We are of good courage, and we would rather be away from the body and at home with the Lord. So whether we are at home or away, we make it our aim to please him" (II Corinthians 5:1-9).

"For this reason I bow my knees before the Father, from whom every family in heaven and on earth is named, that according to the riches of his glory he may grant you to be strengthened with might through his Spirit in the inner man, and that Christ may dwell in your hearts through faith; that you, being rooted and grounded in love, may have power to comprehend with all the saints what is the breadth and length and height and depth, and to know the love of Christ which surpasses knowledge, that you may be filled with all the fulness of God. Now to him who by the power at work within us is able to do far more abundantly than all that we ask or think, to him be glory in the church and in Christ Jesus to all generations, for ever and ever. Amen" (Ephesians 3:14-21).

"Have you not known? Have you not heard? The Lord is the everlasting God, the Creator of the ends of the earth. He does not faint or grow weary, his understanding is unsearchable. He gives power to the faint, and to him who has no might he increases strength. Even youths shall faint and be weary, and young men shall fall exhausted; but they who wait for the Lord shall renew their strength, they shall mount up with wings like eagles, they shall run and not be weary, they shall walk and not faint" (Isaiah 40:28-31).

" 'Oh that my words were written! Oh that they were inscribed in a book! Oh that with an iron pen and lead they were graven in the rock for ever! For I know that my Redeemer lives, and at last he will stand upon the earth; and after my skin has been thus destroyed, then from my flesh I shall see God, whom I shall see on my side, and my eyes shall behold, and not another' " (Job 19:23-27).

"But whatever gain I had, I counted as loss for the sake of Christ. Indeed I count everything as loss because of the surpassing worth of knowing Christ Jesus my Lord. For his sake I have suffered the loss of all things, and count them as refuse, in order that I may gain Christ and be found in him, not having a righteousness of my own, based on law, but that which is through faith in Christ, the righteousness from God that depends on faith; that I may know him and the power of his resurrection, and may share his sufferings, becoming like him in his death, that if possible I may attain the resurrection from the dead. Not that I have already obtained this or am already perfect; but I press on to make it my own, because Christ Jesus has made me his own. Brethren, I do not consider that I have made it my own; but one thing I do, forgetting what lies behind and straining forward to what lies ahead, I press on toward the goal for the prize of the upward call of God in Christ Jesus. Let those of us who are mature be thus minded; and if in anything you are otherwise minded, God will reveal that also to you. Only let us hold true to what we have attained" (Philippians 3:7–16).

"But we would not have you ignorant, brethren, concerning those who are asleep, that you may not grieve as others do who have no hope. For since we believe that Jesus died and rose again, even so, through Jesus, God will bring with him those who have fallen asleep" (I Thessalonians 4:13–14).

For Non-Christians

"Out of the depths I cry to thee, O Lord! Lord, hear my voice! Let thy ears be attentive to the voice of my supplications! If thou, O Lord, shouldst mark iniquities, Lord, who could stand? But there is forgiveness with thee, that thou mayest be feared. I wait for the Lord, my soul waits, and in his word I hope; my soul waits for the Lord more than watchmen for the morning, more than watchmen for the morning. O Israel, hope in the Lord! For with the Lord there is steadfast love, and with him is plenteous redemption. And he will redeem Israel from all his iniquities" (Psalm 130).

"For the grace of God has appeared for the salvation of all men, training us to renounce irreligion and worldly passions, and to live sober, upright, and godly lives in this world, awaiting our blessed hope, the appearing of the glory of our great God and Savior Jesus Christ, who gave himself for us to redeem us from all iniquity and to purify for himself a people of his own who are zealous for good deeds" (Titus 2:11–14).

PASTORAL PRAYERS

O Thou who hast made no life in vain, and who lovest all that Thou hast made: we bow in gratitude for the life of the departed one in whose memory we are met. Recall to our minds the relationships which have made this life meaningful to us, and for those qualities beyond physical dimensions that we have experienced in him.

O Father of mercy and goodness, whose nature is love: release the feelings of remorse, with the knowledge that Thou dost love us in spite of our shortcomings, so we can love and forgive ourselves for deeds done and undone. Remove any feelings of resentment toward anyone by the memory of our Lord, who forgave and loved even those who misused and abused Him. Grant to these upon whom this death comes, the ability to face the reality of loss, to accept the fact without escape, and to assimilate it into their lives so that they can live usefully and normally, as Thou wouldst have them.

O Thou who art from everlasting to everlasting, the *Alpha* and the *Omega* of all things: Deepen our faith in Thee, O God, and in Thy provisions for life beyond death, through Jesus Christ. Support with Thy church's fellowship, these friends, and bind the hearts of the family with the bonds of Christian love, until the morning dawns and the shadows flee away.

O Thou who art the Lord of Life and the Conqueror of Death: Help us to know that we are spiritual beings living in a spiritual universe, so we need not fear death. Help us to believe that while the things that are seen pass away, and that things that are unseen are real and eternal, so we need not despair. Help us to realize the new spiritual life in Christ, which death cannot take away and the grave cannot destroy. With this assurance we find comfort and peace.

O Thou Source of all good, we thank Thee for the goodness in our *brother,* for *his* experience of Thy redeeming grace, for *his* faithfulness in all relationships. The passing of every faithful spirit brings us more closely to that inheritance which is undefiled, incorruptible, and reserved in Heaven for all who love Thee, through Jesus Christ. Amen.

Eternal Spirit from whose womb of nature we have come to being, and unto whom we return: in Thine everlastingness and love we rely. There is none other to whom we can turn. Thou art the One everlasting to everlasting, the *Alpha* and the *Omega.* How majestic is Thy name in all the earth!

In these moments that shake us emotionally and try us spiritually, tie our faith to Jesus Christ, who revealed the kind of life that pleases Thee, is confirmed with resurrection, and rewarded with eternalness.

Relieve with an assurance of Thy forgiveness, feelings of remorse and guilt over what we have done that we should not have done, and things we have left undone that we should have done. In the knowledge that Thou dost forgive and love us still, Merciful Father, may we find ability to forgive ourselves.

We commend to Thy keeping this one, rich in good works. Sanctify to us *his* memory. Help us to continue here to serve Thee with constancy, until our summons comes; then may we be united with Thy blessed ones, through Jesus Christ, our Lord. Amen.

Infinite mind of God, whose Holy Word has communicated Thy thoughts, love, and truth to our human minds: We thank Thee for the strengthening power and comfort, derived from the reading and interpretation of Holy Scripture.

We are grateful, Father of Mercy, for Thy promise in the words of the Psalmist, who said, "The Lord is nigh unto all them that call upon him. . . ." Grant us to know that we are not outside Thy presence or attention.

We thank Thee, gracious Father, for Thy assurance in the words of Paul, who said, "My God shall supply every need of yours according to his riches in glory in Christ." How great is our need. How comforting to know Thy power to supply is even greater.

We thank Thee, Father of Love, for the words from the lips of our Saviour, Jesus Christ, who said, "Let not your hearts be troubled . . . I go to prepare a place for you . . . I will come again and receive you." With such provision and companionship, we are not fearful or troubled.

With this revelation, we face the future confident and assured. Amen.

Our Heavenly Father, who art waiting to receive and answer each sincere and simple prayer, we turn to Thee in our great need, asking for light in our darkness and deliverance from our doubts and fears. Thou sendest forth thy breath, we are created; thou takest away our life, we die and return to the dust. Whether we live, then, or die, we are in Thy compassionate and loving care; and the shadow that darkens our path is but the close-approaching, overbrooding shadow of Thy nearer presence.

Here, we commit to Thy unfailing love the beloved soul now departed. We thank Thee for the gracious memories which gather about this life, for kindly deeds and thoughts, for the love freely given and the love modestly received, for the patient bearing of the heavy cross of solitude and pain, and now at last for quiet release from the burden of the flesh and entrance into the peace reserved for those who love Thee. The Lord gave, and the Lord hath taken away; blessed be the name of the Lord.[1] Amen.

Eternal Spirit, Father of our spirits, from whom we have come, to whom we belong, and in whose fellowship is our peace: we turn to Thee. Amid the turmoil of emotion and the loneliness of loss, remind us of all the spiritual assets that have blessed our lives. Refresh in us the first loves that made our families. Kindle anew in us the beauty of parental relationships and the ties of blood. Strengthen the bonds of our friendships which add comfort and enlarge vision. May the fellowship of the churches *she* has served surround *her* with a great cloud of witnesses, confirming faith and bolstering courage. When knowledge questions *why* and sight is dim, tie our faith to Jesus Christ, who opened up the shades so we can view the horizon and find the way.

Heavenly Father, we thank Thee for every remembrance of our departed: for the qualities of personality that endeared her to us all; for the unselfish service rendered to Thy Kingdom; for the mother's love which fortified her children; and for the devoted companionship in the ministry. Into Thy eternal presence we commend her keeping.

We pray for those upon whom this death so closely comes. May they be comforted with the same comfort wherewith we have been comforted—the knowledge that love does not lose its own; the assurance of forgiveness for neglect; the promise of a glad reunion day; and the certainty that Thou dost work in all things for good to those who love Thee, through Jesus Christ, our Lord. Amen.

QUOTABLE POEMS

CROSSING THE BAR

Sunset and evening star,
  And one clear call for me!
And may there be no moaning at the bar
  When I put out to sea.

But such a tide as moving seems asleep,
  Too full for sound and foam,
When that which drew from out the boundless deep,
  Turns again home.

Twilight and evening bell,
  And after that the dark!
And may there be no sadness of farewell
  When I embark.

For though from out our bourne of Time and Place,
  The flood may bear me far,
I hope to see my Pilot face to face,
  When I have crossed the bar.

—Alfred Tennyson

TO A WATERFOWL

He who, from zone to zone,
Guides through the boundless sky thy certain flight,
In the long way that I must tread alone,
  Will lead my steps aright.

—William Cullen Bryant

121

THE ETERNAL GOODNESS

I see the wrong that round me lies,
    I feel the guilt within;
I hear, with groan and travail-cries,
    The world confess its sin.

Yet, in the maddening maze of things,
    And tossed by storm and flood,
To one fixed trust my spirit clings;
    I know that God is good!

I long for household voices gone,
    For vanished smiles I long,
But God hath led my dear ones on,
    And He can do no wrong.

I know not what the future hath
    Of marvel or surprise,
Assured alone that life and death
    His mercy underlies.

And so beside the Silent Sea
    I wait the muffled oar;
No harm from Him can come to me
    On ocean or on shore.

I know not where His islands lift
    Their fronded palms in air;
I only know I cannot drift
    Beyond His love and care.
           —*John Greenleaf Whittier*

COME, YE DISCONSOLATE

Come, ye disconsolate, wher'er you languish,
    Come, at God's altar fervently kneel;
Here bring your wounded hearts, here tell your anguish—
    Earth has no sorrow that Heaven cannot heal.

Joy of the desolate, Light of the straying,
    Hope, when all others die, fadeless and pure,
Here speaks the Comforter, in God's name saying—
    "Earth has no sorrow that Heaven cannot heal."
           —*Thomas Moore*

FROM *RENASCENCE* (conclusion)

The world stands out on either side
No wider than the heart is wide;
Above the world is stretched the sky,
No higher than the soul is high.

The heart can push the sea and land
Farther away on either hand;
The soul can split the sky in two,
And let the face of God shine through.

But East and West will pinch the heart
That can not keep them pushed apart;
And he whose soul is flat—the sky
Will cave in on him by and by.
                    —*Edna St. Vincent Millay*

THE THOROUGHBRED

We come into this life all naked and bare.
We go through this life with worry and care,
We go from this life, we know not where,
But if you are a thoroughbred here,
You will be a thoroughbred there.
                    —*Anonymous*

THE REDEEMED IN GLORY

From North and South, and East and West,
     They come!
The sorely tried, the much oppressed,
Their Faith and Love to manifest,
     They come!
They come to tell of work well done,
They come to tell of kingdoms won,
To worship at the Great White Throne,
     They come!
In a noble consecration,
With a sound of jubilation,
       They come! They come!
                    —*John Oxenham*

123

TEN THOUSAND TIMES TEN THOUSAND

Ten Thousand times ten thousand
    In sparkling raiment bright,
The armies of the ransomed saints
    Throng up the steeps of light:
'Tis finished! all is finished,
    Their fight with death and sin:
Fling open wide the golden gates,
    And let the victors in.

What rush of alleluias
    Fills all the earth and sky!
What ringing of a thousand harps
    Bespeaks the triumph nigh!
O day, for which creation
    And all its tribes were made!
O joy, for all its former woes
    A thousand-fold repaid!

O then what raptured greetings
    On Canaan's happy shore!
What knitting severed friendships up,
    Where partings are no more!
Then eyes with joy shall sparkle
    That brimmed with tears of late;
Orphans no longer fatherless,
    Nor widows desolate.

Bring near thy great salvation,
    Thou Lamb for sinners slain;
Fill up the roll of thine elect,
    Then take thy power and reign!
Appear, Desire of nations!
    Thine exiles long for home:
Show in the heavens thy promised sign!
    Thou Prince and Saviour, come!
        —Henry Alford

NOW THE LABORER'S TASK IS O'ER

Now the laborer's task is o'er;
    Now the battle day is past;
Now upon the farther shore
    Lands the voyager at last.

Father, in thy gracious keeping
Leave we now thy servant sleeping.

There the tears of earth are dried;
    There its hidden things are clear;
There the work of life is tried
    By a juster Judge than here.
Father, in thy gracious keeping
Leave we now thy servant sleeping.

There the sinful souls, that turn
    To the cross their dying eyes,
All the love of Christ shall learn
    At his feet in Paradise.
Father, in thy gracious keeping
Leave we now thy servant sleeping.

"Earth to earth, and dust to dust,"
    Calmly now the words we say;
Left behind, we wait in trust
    For the resurrection day.
Father, in thy gracious keeping
Leave we now thy servant sleeping.
                —John Ellerton

THE WEAVER

My life is but a weaving
    Between my Lord and me;
I may not choose the colors,
    He knows what they should be;
For He can view the pattern
    Upon the upper side,
While I can see it only
    On this, the under side.

Sometimes He weaveth sorrow,
    Which seems strange to me;
But I will trust His judgment,
    And work as faithfully;
'Tis He who fills the shuttle,
    He knows just what is best,
So I shall weave in earnest
    And leave with Him the rest.

Not till the loom is silent
  And the shuttles cease to fly
Shall God unroll the canvas
  And explain the reason why—
The dark threads are as needful
  In the weaver's skillful hand
As the threads of gold and silver
  In the pattern He has planned.
                    —*Anonymous*

MY DEAD

I cannot think of them as dead
  Who walk with me no more;
Along the path of life I tread
  They have but gone before.

The Father's house is mansioned fair
  Beyond my vision dim;
All souls are his, and here or there
  Are living unto him.

And still their silent ministry
  Within my heart hath place,
As when on earth they walked with me
  And met me face to face.

Their lives are made forever mine;
  What they to me have been
Hath left henceforth its seal and sign
  Engraven deep within.

Mine are they by an ownership
  Nor time nor death can free;
For God hath given to Love to keep
  Its own eternally.
                    —*Frederick L. Hosmer*

ONE SWEETLY SOLEMN THOUGHT

One sweetly solemn thought
  Comes to me o'er and o'er;
Nearer my home today am I
  Than e'er I've been before.

Nearer my Father's house,
    Where many mansions be;
Nearer, today, the great white throne,
    Nearer the crystal sea.

Nearer the bound of life,
    Where burdens are laid down;
Nearer, to leave the heavy cross
    Nearer to gain the crown.

But, lying dark between,
    Winding down through the night,
There rolls the deep and unknown stream
    That leads at last to light.

E'en now, perchance, my feet
    Are slipping on the brink,
And I, today, am nearer home,—
    Nearer than now I think.

Father, perfect my trust!
    Strengthen my power of faith!
Nor let me stand, at last, alone
    Upon the shore of death.
                    —*Phoebe Cary*

IN MEMORIAM

Forgive my grief for one removed,
    Thy creature, whom I found so fair.
    I trust he lives in thee, and there
I find him worthier to be loved.

Forgive these wild and wandering cries,
    Confusions of a wasted youth;
    Forgive them where they fail in truth,
And in thy wisdom make me wise.
                    —*Alfred Tennyson*

EMANCIPATION

Why be afraid of death
As though your life were breath?
    Death but anoints your eyes
    With clay, O glad surprise!

127

Why should you be forlorn?
Death only husks the corn.
  Why should you fear to meet
  The Thresher of the wheat?
Is sleep a thing to dread?
Yet, sleeping you are dead
  Till you awake and rise,
  Here, or beyond the skies.
Why should it be a wrench
To leave your wooden bench?
  Why not, with happy shout,
  Run home when school is out?
The dear ones left behind?
O foolish one and blind,
  A day, and you will meet;
  A night, and you will greet.
This is the death of death:
To breathe away a breath,
  And know the end of strife,
  And taste the deathless life,
And joy without a fear,
And smile without a tear,
  And work, nor care nor rest,
  And find the last the best.
                    —*Maltbie D. Babcock*

FAREWELL IN AUTUMN

Not in winter, not in storm,
Nor when spring's buds are calling,
But in autumn's quiet charm,
While russet leaves are falling.
The good earth turns herself to rest,
After her time of growing,
Drawing her children to her breast,
To wait a richer sowing.
So in his autumn's golden day,
His earthly life forsaking,
In quiet peace he passed away,
To meet the last awaking.
                    —*Will C. Osborn*

MYSTERY

What is this mystery that men call death?
My friend before me lies; in all save breath
He seems the same as yesterday. His face
So like to life, so calm, bears not a trace
Of that great change which all of us so dread.
I gaze on him and say: He is not dead,
But sleeps; and soon he will arise and take
Me by the hand. I know he will awake
And smile on me as he did yesterday;
And he will have some gentle word to say
Some kindly deed to do; for loving thought
Was warp and woof of which his life was wrought.
He is not dead. Such souls forever live
In boundless measure of the love they give.

—Jerome B. Bell[2]

A SONG OF THANKSGIVING

Saints are God's flowers, fragrant souls
    That His own hand hath planted,
Not in some far-off heavenly place,
    Or solitude enchanted,
But here and there and everywhere,—
    In lonely field, or crowded town,
    God sees a flower when He looks down.

One such I knew,—and had the grace
    To thank my God for knowing:
The beauty of her quiet life
    Was like a rose in blowing,
So fair and sweet, so all-complete
    And all unconscious, as a flower,
    That light and fragrance were her dower.

A vow to keep her life alive
    In deeds of pure affection,
So that her love shall find in them
    A daily resurrection;
A constant prayer that they may wear
    Some touch of that supernal light
    With which she blossoms in God's sight.

—Henry van Dyke

IN ANOTHER ROOM

No, not cold beneath the grasses,
    Not close-walled within the tomb;
Rather, in our Father's mansion,
    Living, in another room.

Living, like the man who loves me,
    Like my child with cheeks abloom,
Out of sight, at desk or schoolbook,
    Busy, in another room.

Nearer than my son whom fortune
    Beckons where the strange lands loom;
Just behind the hanging curtain,
    Serving, in another room.

Shall I doubt my Father's mercy?
    Shall I think of death as doom,
Or the stepping o'er the threshold
    To a bigger, brighter room?

Shall I blame my Father's wisdom?
    Shall I sit enswathed in gloom,
When I know my loves are happy,
    Waiting in another room?
            —*Robert Freeman*

RABBI BEN EZRA

Grow old along with me!
The best is yet to be,
The last of life, for which the first was made:
Our times are in his hand
Who saith, "A whole I planned,
Youth shows but half; trust God: see all, nor be afraid!"

All that is at all,
Lasts ever, past recall;
Earth changes, but thy soul and God stand sure:
What entered into thee,
That was, is, and shall be:
Time's wheel runs back or stops: Potter and clay endure.

So, take and use thy work:
Amend what flaws may lurk,

130

What strain o' the stuff, what warpings past the aim!
My times be in thy hand!
Perfect the cup as planned!
Let age approve of youth, and death complete the same!
—*Robert Browning*

A MOTHER'S FAREWELL

Dear Lord, receive my son, whose winning love
To me was like a friendship, far above
The course of nature or his tender age,
Whose looks could all my bitter griefs assuage;
Let his pure soul ordained sev'n years to be
In that frail body, which was part of me,
Remain my pledge in Heav'n, as sent to show
How to this port with ev'ry step I go.
—*John Beaumont*[3]

THE OPEN DOOR

You, my son,
Have shown me God.
Your kiss upon my cheek
Has made me feel the gentle touch
Of him who leads us on.
The memory of your smile, when young,
Reveals his face,
As mellowing years come on apace.
And when you went before,
You left the gates of heaven ajar
That I might glimpse,
Approaching from afar,
The glories of his grace.
Hold, son, my hand,
Guide me along the path,
That, coming,
I may stumble not
Nor roam,
Nor fail to show the way
Which leads us—home.
—*Grace Coolidge (written in memory*
of Calvin Coolidge, Jr., on the fifth
anniversary of his death)[4]

OF SUCH IS THE KINGDOM

My darling boy, so early snatched away
    From arms still seeking thee in empty air,
That thou shouldst come to me I do not pray,
    Lest, by thy coming, heaven should be less fair.

Stay, rather, in perennial flower of youth,
    Such as the Master, looking on, must love;
And send to me the spirit of the truth,
    To teach me of the wisdom from above.

Beckon to guide my thoughts, as stumblingly
    They seek the kingdom of the undefiled;
And meet me at its gateway with thy key,
    The unstained spirit of a little child.
                —*Francis Greenwood Peabody*[5]

BABY SLEEPS

    The baby wept;
The mother took it from the nurse's arms,
And hushed its fears, and soothed its vain alarms,
    And baby slept.

    Again it weeps,
And God doth take it from the mother's arms,
From present griefs, and future unknown harms,
    And baby sleeps.
                —*Samuel Hinds*[6]

THE HOMELAND!

The Homeland! O the Homeland!
    The land of souls freeborn!
No gloomy night is known there,
    But eye the fadeless morn:
I'm sighing for that country,
    My heart is aching here;
There is no pain in the Homeland
    To which I'm drawing near.

My Lord is in the Homeland,
    With angels bright and fair;
No sinful thing nor evil,
    Can ever enter there;

The music of the ransomed
    Is ringing in my ears,
And when I think of the Homeland,
    My eyes are wet with tears.

For loved ones in the Homeland
    Are waiting me to come
Where neither death nor sorrow
    Invades their holy home:
O dear, dear native country!
    O rest and peace above!
Christ bring us all to the Homeland
    Of his eternal love.
          —*Hugh R. Haweis*

THE MEANING OF DEATH

We are so stupid about death. We will not learn
How it is wages paid to those who earn,
How it is gift for which on earth we yearn,
To be set free from bondage to the flesh;
How it is turning seed-corn into grain,
How it is winning heaven's eternal gain,
How it means freedom ever more from pain.
    How it untangles every mortal mesh.

We are so selfish about death, we count our grief
Far more than we consider their relief
Whom the great Reaper gathers in the sheaf
No more to know the season's constant change:
And we forget that it means only life.
          —*William C. Doane*

O PARADISE, O PARADISE

O Paradise, O Paradise,
    Who doth not crave for rest?
Who would not seek the happy land
    Where they that loved are blest?

Refrain:
Where loyal hearts and true
    Stand ever in the light,
All rapture, through and through,
    In God's most holy sight.

O Paradise, O Paradise,
  The world is growing old;
Who would not be at rest and free
  Where love is never cold?

O Paradise, O Paradise,
  We long to sin no more;
We long to be as pure on earth
  As on thy spotless shore;

O Paradise, O paradise,
  We shall not wait for long;
E'en now the loving ear may catch
  Faint fragments of thy song;

Lord Jesus, King of Paradise,
  O keep us in thy love,
And guide us to that happy land
  Of perfect rest above.
        —*Frederick William Faber*

THE ROSE STILL GROWS BEYOND THE WALL

Near shady wall a rose once grew,
  Budded and blossomed in God's free light,
Watered and fed by morning dew,
  Shedding its sweetness day and night.

As it grew and blossomed, fair and tall,
  Slowly rising to loftier height,
It came to a crevice in the wall,
  Through which there shone a beam of light.

Onward it crept with added strength,
  With never a thought of fear or pride,
It followed the light through the crevice's length
  And unfolded itself on the other side.

The light, the dew, the broadening view,
  Were found the same as they were before:
And it lost itself in beauties new,
  Breathing its fragrance more and more.

Shall claim of death cause us to grieve,
  And make our courage faint or fall?
Nay, let us faith and hope receive:
  The rose still grows beyond the wall,

Scattering fragrance far and wide,
    Just as it did in days of yore,
Just as it did on the other side,
    Just as it will for evermore.
                —*A. L. Frink*[7]

THE TWO SHIPS

As I stand by the cross on the lone mountain's crest,
    Looking over the ultimate sea,
In the gloom of the mountain a ship lies at rest,
    And one sails away from the lea:
One spreads its white wings on a far reaching track,
    With pennant and sheet flowing free:
One hides in the shadow with sails laid back—
    The ship is waiting for me!

But lo! In the distance the clouds break away
    The gate's glowing portals see:
And I hear from the outgoing ship in the bay
    The song of the sailors in glee.
So I think of the luminous footprints that bore
    The comfort o'er dark Galilee,
And wait for the signal to go to the shore,
    To the ship that is waiting for me.
                —*Bret Harte*[8]

THE DYING CHRISTIAN TO HIS SOUL

Vital spark of heavenly flame!
Quit, O quit this mortal frame;
Trembling, hoping, lingering, flying,
O the pain, the bliss of dying!
Cease, fond Nature, cease thy strife,
And let me languish into life!

The world recedes; it disappears!
Heaven opens on my eyes! my ears
With sounds seraphic ring!
Lend, lend your wings! I mount! I fly!
O Grave! where is thy victory?
O Death! where is thy sting?
             —*Alexander Pope*

". . . [May] the God of our Lord Jesus Christ, the Father of glory . . . give you a spirit of wisdom and of revelation in the knowledge of him . . ." (Ephesians 1:17).

"Blessed be the God and Father of our Lord Jesus Christ, who has blessed us in Christ with every spiritual blessing in the heavenly places . . ." (Ephesians 1:3).

". . . to the only God, our Savior through Jesus Christ our Lord, be glory, majesty, dominion, and authority, before all time and now and for ever. Amen" (Jude 25).

"The Lord bless you and keep you: The Lord make his face to shine upon you, and be gracious to you: The Lord lift up his countenance upon you, and give you peace" (Numbers 6:24–26).

GOD WALKS IN THE GARDEN

God walks in the garden,
And the gloom and the dark
Change to the lights
Of a heavenly park.
God walks in the garden
And the delicate hues
Of iris and jonquil
And the brittle blues
Of harebell and larkspur
Mingle and blend
In a glorious pattern
Which has no end.
God walks in the garden—
He treads up and down;
And each bud and blossom
Lifts a star-crown
Fragile, filigreed
But of infinite worth
To Him who fashioned
This beautiful earth.
—*Margie B. Boswell*
(in *Wings Against the Dawn*)

IMMORTAL GUEST

The soul on earth is an immortal guest,
Compelled to starve at an unreal feast;
A spark which upward tends by nature's force,
A stream divided from its parent source,
A drop dissevered from the boundless sea,
A moment parted from eternity,
A pilgrim panting for the rest to come;
An exile anxious for his native home.
—*Hannah More*

HOW BEAUTIFUL TO BE WITH GOD!

How beautiful to be with God,
When earth is fading like a dream,
And from this mist-encircled shore
We launch upon the unknown stream!

139

No doubt, no fear, no anxious care,
    But comforted by staff and rod,
In the faith-brightened hour of death
    How beautiful to be be with God!

Beyond the partings and the pains,
    Beyond the sighing and the tears,
Oh, beautiful to be with God
    Through all the endless, blessed years—
To see His face, to hear His voice,
    To know Him better day by day,
And love Him as the flowers love light,
    And serve Him as immortals may.
                —*Author Unknown*

GOOD NIGHT

Warm summer sun,
    Shine kindly here.
Warm southern wind,
    Blow softly here.
Green sod above,
    Lie light, lie light,
Good night, dear heart,
    Good night, good night.
           —*Robert Richardson*[1]

UNTIL TOMORROW

According to the eternal plan,
    The body returns to the earth as it was,
And the spirit to God who gave it.
    Of all that is material we say,
"Earth to earth, ashes to ashes, dust to dust";
    But to the spirit we cry:
"Now thou art free,
    Free from pain and sickness and sorrow.
Free from all physical handicaps,
    Free to dream and sing and work and love.
Free to greet old friends and new
    And Jesus Christ,
And to adventure with them forever."
    Therefore we say,
"Good-bye, good-bye until tomorrow." Amen.
           Chauncey R. Piety[2]

THANATOPSIS

So live, that when thy summons comes to join
    The innumerable caravan, which moves
To that mysterious realm, where each shall take
    His chamber in the silent halls of death,
Thou go not, like a quarry-slave at night,
    Scourged to his dungeon, but, sustained and soothed
By an unfaltering trust, approach thy grave
    Like one who wraps the drapery of his couch
About him and lies down to pleasant dreams.
                    —*William Cullen Bryant*

O HAPPY SOUL

O happy soul, be thankful now, and rest!
    Heaven is a goodly land;
And God is love; and those he loves are blest;
    Now thou dost understand
The least thou hast is better than the best
That thou didst hope for; now upon thine eyes
    The new life opens fair;
Before thy feet the blessed journey lies
    Through homelands everywhere;
And heaven to thee is all a sweet surprise.
                    —*Washington Gladden*[3]

WELL DONE

Servant of God, well done!
    Rest from thy loved employ:
The battle fought, the victory won,
    Enter thy Master's joy.
The pains of death are past,
    Labour and sorrow cease,
And Life's long warfare closed at last,
    Thy soul is found in peace.
                    —*James Montgomery*[4]

REQUIEM

Under the wide and starry sky,
Dig the grave and let me lie.
Glad did I live and gladly die,
    And I laid me down with a will.

This be the verse you grave for me:
Here he lies where he longed to be;
Home is the sailor, home from sea,
    And the hunter home from the hill.
        —Robert Louis Stevenson

THE ETERNAL VOYAGE

Is this the end? I know it cannot be.
Our ships shall sail upon another sea;
New islands yet shall break upon our sight,
New continents of love and truth and might.
        —John White Chadwick[5]

SEEDS

We drop a seed into the ground,
A tiny, shapeless thing, shrivelled and dry,
And, in the fulness of its time, is seen
A form of peerless beauty, robed and crowned
Beyond the pride of any earthly queen,
Instinct with loveliness, and sweet and rare,
The perfect emblem of its Maker's care.

This from a shrivelled seed?—
—Then may man hope indeed!

For man is but the seed of what he shall be,
When, in the fulness of his perfecting,
He drops the husk and cleaves his upward way,
Through earth's retardings and the clinging clay,
Into the sunshine of God's perfect day.
No fetters then! No bonds of time or space!
But powers as ample as the boundless grace
That suffered man, and death, and yet in tenderness,
Set wide the door, and passed Himself before—
As He had promised—to prepare a place.

We know not what we shall be—only this—
That we shall be made like Him—as He is.
        —John Oxenham[6]

142

IN HARDWOOD GROVES

The same leaves over and over again!
They fall from giving shade above
To make one texture of faded brown
And fit the earth like a leather glove.

Before the leaves can mount again
To fill the trees with another shade,
They must go down past things coming up,
They must go down into the dark decayed.

They must be pierced by flowers and put
Beneath the feet of dancing flowers,
However it is in some other world
I know that this is the way in ours.

—*Robert Frost*[7]

THE APOSTLES' CREED (Optional)

I believe in God the Father Almighty, Maker of heaven and earth:
And in Jesus Christ his only Son our Lord: Who was conceived
by the Holy Ghost, Born of the Virgin Mary: Suffered under Pontius
Pilate, Was crucified, dead, and buried: He descended into hell; The
third day he rose again from the dead: He ascended into heaven,
And sitteth on the right hand of God the Father Almighty: From
thence he shall come to judge the quick and the dead.

I believe in the Holy Ghost: The holy Catholic Church; The Communion of Saints: The Forgiveness of sins: The Resurrection of the
body: And the Life everlasting. Amen.

WORDS OF COMMITTAL

At Grave

FOR A BELIEVER

Into the gracious keeping of God, our Help in ages past, our Hope
for years to come, we commit the soul of our departed *brother*, grateful for all that *he* has meant to us, and praying that through the grace
of our Lord, Jesus Christ, *he* may be granted an abundant entrance
into the eternal kingdom. Here in this place, with its tender associations, we dedicate ourselves anew to God's service, that, with chastened
desires and nobler motives, we may return to our homes and the duties
that await us, to glorify our Lord, Jesus Christ.

Cherishing memories which are forever sacred, sustained by a faith that is stronger than death, comforted by the hope of a life that endless shall be, all that is mortal of our friend we therefore commit to its resting place, amidst these beautiful surroundings of nature, in the assurance that if the earthly house of our tabernacle be dissolved, we have a building from God, a house not made with hands, eternal in the heavens.

I heard a voice from heaven: "Write, 'blessed are the dead which die in the Lord' from henceforth; yea," saith the Spirit, "that they may rest from their labors; and their works do follow them."

FOR AN UNBELIEVER

In this solemn hour we commit to the ground the body of our beloved ~~friend~~, and present to God's mercy and gracious care his spirit. May we rededicate ourselves to God, and obtain grace for all that is to come, until the day break, and these shadows flee away.

Freed at last from all the tensions, confusions, and limitations of this mortal life, we pray that all the aspirations and prayers of our beloved may be multiplied in power by infinity, and that all the love-liest wishes of our departed one may come to pass in glorious fulfill-ment for all the loved ones left behind and for the benefits of God's children everywhere. (Adapted from Glenn Clark)

Here we commit the body to its kindred dust. The spirit we leave with God. May the living take it to heart. As we know that God will bring us everyone to the grave, let us here dedicate ourselves to do with our might what our hands find to do. May our trust be in Him who said, "I am the resurrection and the life; he that believeth in me, though he were dead, yet shall he live; and whosoever liveth and believeth in me shall never die."

At Mausoleum

> Within this mansion of the dead
>   We lay a form to rest,
> A form a friend has tenanted
>   And love and joy have blest.
>
> The body shall return to dust
>   According to the Word,
> The spirit fellowships the just
>   And Jesus Christ, our Lord.

Though Death reign here in stern array,
    Our faith to God we give:
While steel and stone and flesh decay,
    The soul with him shall live.

So we commit us all to God,
    Master of death and change,
And He will bring us to our friends
    Through loving ways and strange.
                    Amen.[8]
            —*Chauncey R. Piety*

At Columbarium

IF BEFORE CREMATION

Forasmuch as it hath pleased God to take unto Himself the soul of our *brother* here departed, we therefore commit *his* body to be dissolved . . . in sure and certain hope of eternal life through our Lord, Jesus Christ.

IF CREMATION HAS ALREADY TAKEN PLACE

Forasmuch as it hath pleased God to take unto Himself the soul of our *brother* here departed, we therefore commit *his* ashes to this resting place . . . in sure and certain hope of eternal life through our Lord, Jesus Christ.

(The wise minister will never make any reference to "fire" or "burning" if cremation is the method of disposal. He will have to use his best intuitive wisdom in adapting for the slightly different situations. If in doubt, he should counsel with the funeral director regarding what is appropriate or customary in procedure.)

At Sea

Poem: *Sunset and Evening Star* (page 121)

Forasmuch as it has pleased Almighty God to take out of the world the soul of our departed *brother*, we therefore commit *his* body to the deep; looking to life eternal through our Lord Jesus Christ at whose coming in glorious majesty, the moaning sea shall give up her dead; our mortal bodies shall be made like unto His glorious body, and the sea shall be no more.

Pastoral Prayers

At Grave

Heavenly Father, look in mercy upon these our friends as they leave the earthly form of their loved one resting beneath the beauty of Thy flowers. Be with these Thy children as they go again to their homes. Grant them faith to believe in the communion of saints, the forgiveness of sins, the resurrection of the body, and the life everlasting. Through Thy Spirit, enable them to be steadfast, unmovable, always abounding in the work of the Lord, forasmuch as they know that their labor is not in vain in the Lord. Amen.[9]

O Lord, Jesus Christ, who did Thyself weep beside the grave and art touched with the feelings of our sorrows, fulfill now Thy promise that Thou wilt not leave Thy people comfortless, but will come to them. Help them to hear Thee saying, "I am the resurrection and the life. . . . Because I live, you shall live also." In faith may they find God's presence to sustain them now, and a sure confidence in Thee for all that is to come, until the day break, and these shadows flee away—world without end. Amen.

At Columbarium or Mausoleum

Almighty God, who by the resurrection of Thy Son destroyed death and assured victory: Grant that these bereaved may not sorrow as those without hope. In thankful remembrance of Thy great goodness in past years, and the expectation of a joyful reunion in heavenly places, may they find strength to meet the days to come with steadfastness and courage, in the name of Jesus Christ, who brought life and immortality to light.

Our Father, who art in heaven, Hallowed be thy Name. Thy kingdom come. Thy will be done, On earth as it is in heaven. Give us this day our daily bread. And forgive us our debts, As we also have forgiven our debtors. And lead us not into temptation, But deliver us from evil. For thine is the kingdom, and the power, and the glory, forever. Amen.

BENEDICTIONS

"Now may the God of peace who brought again from the dead our Lord Jesus, the great shepherd of the sheep, by the blood of the eternal covenant, equip you with everything good that you may do his will, working in you that which is pleasing in his sight, through Jesus Christ; to whom be glory for ever and ever. Amen." (Hebrew 13:20, 21).

146

"The Lord bless you and keep you: The Lord make his face to shine upon you, and be gracious to you: The Lord lift up his countenance upon you, and give you peace" (Numbers 6:24–26).

". . . thanks be to God, who gives us the victory through our Lord, Jesus Christ" (I Corinthians 15:57).

"Now to him who by the power at work within us is able to do far more abundantly than all that we ask or think, to him be glory in the church and in Christ Jesus to all generations, for ever and ever. Amen." (Ephesians 3:20).

". . . the peace of God, which passes all understanding, will keep your hearts and your minds in Christ Jesus" (Philippians 4:7).

INTERMENT SERVICE FOR A CHILD

Scriptures

"Lord, thou hast been our dwelling place in all generations. Before the mountains were brought forth, or ever thou hadst formed the earth and the world, from everlasting to everlasting thou art God" (Psalm 90:1–2).

"Blessed be the God and Father of our Lord Jesus Christ, the Father of mercies and God of all comfort, who comforts us in all our affliction, so that we may be able to comfort those who are in any affliction, with the comfort with which we ourselves are comforted by God" (II Corinthians 1:3–4).

Appropriate Poem

O HAPPY SOUL

O happy soul, be thankful now, and rest!
    Heaven is a goodly land;
And God is love; and those he loves are blest;
    Now thou dost understand
The least thou hast is better than the best
That thou didst hope for; now upon thine eyes
    The new life opens fair;
Before thy feet the blessed journey lies
    Through homelands everywhere;
And heaven to thee is all a sweet surprise.
          —*Washington Gladden*[10]

147

Prayer

Loving and compassionate Father, whose Son did take little children in His arms, bless them, and say, "Of such is the Kingdom of Heaven," we commit to Thy love this child of these parents' love. ~~In the happy company of the glorified children, nurture~~ *him,* ~~and when the mystery of Thy providence shall be unveiled, restore~~ *him* ~~to these yearning hearts.~~ Sustain them with remembrance of the joys of anticipating this one's arrival, and with the expectation of joyful reunion in life's heavenly places, through Jesus Christ, the Eternal Shepherd and our Comforter. Amen.

Benediction

The Peace of God, which passeth all understanding, keep your hearts and minds in the knowledge and love of God, and of His Son Jesus Christ our Lord: And the Blessing of God Almighty, the Father, the Son, and the Holy Ghost, be amongst you, and remain with you always. Amen.

NOTES

CHAPTER I

1. Andrew Blackwood, *The Funeral* (Westminster Press, Phila., Pa., 1942), page 53.
2. Dr. William E. Orchard.
3. John Henry Newman.
4. Andrew Blackwood, op. cit., page 50.

CHAPTER III

1. Norman Vincent Peale, Inspirational Book Service.

CHAPTER IV

1. Richard Burton, "If We Had the Time" (Lothrop, Lee and Shepard Co., N.Y.).
2. James Phillip Bailey, "We Live in Deeds," from *Festus.*
3. Ralph Sockman, *Higher Happiness* (Abingdon Press, 1950), page 62.
4. Edgar Guest, "I'll Lend You for a Little While," *To All Parents*, page 60.
5. Author Unknown.
6. Author Unknown.
7. Andrew Blackwood, op. cit., by John Watson, page 245.
8. Author Unknown.
9. Henry F. Lyte.
10. George Matheson.

CHAPTER V

1. John Todd.
2. Charles L. Wallis, *The Funeral Encyclopedia* (Harper and Row, N.Y.), "The Victor" by Thomas Curtis Clark.
3. Henry Alford.
4. Josephine Lemmonds.
5. Douglas Mollock.

6. James Phillip Bailey, "We Live in Deeds," from *Festus*.
7. Charles L. Wallis, op. cit., by Elma Dean.
8. Author Unknown.
9. John Greenleaf Whittier, from *Poems for the Great Days* (Clark and Clark, Abingdon Press, N.Y., 1948).
10. Henry Wadsworth Longfellow.
11. A. L. Alexander, *Poems That Touch the Heart*, poem by Cortlandt W. Sayres, page 28.
12. Rudyard Kipling.
13. Maurie Clay, from *Best Loved Religious Poems* (Fleming H. Revell Co., Westwood, N.J.).
14. Charles L. Wallis, op. cit., by Robert Stephens, page 205.
15. Ibid, by James Montgomery.

CHAPTER VI

1. Alice Freeman Palmer, *A Marriage Cycle* (Houghton Mifflin Company).
2. Oliver Wendell Holmes.
3. Charles L. Wallis, op. cit., by John White Chadwick.
4. Ibid, G. A. Studdert Kennedy, "The Kiss of God."

CHAPTER VIII

1. Charles Wallis, op. cit., by Frances Greenwood Peabody.
2. James Dalton Morrison, *Masterpieces of Religious Verse*, permission granted by Charles L. Wallis for poem "Mystery" by Jerome B. Bell.
3. Charles L. Wallis, op. cit., "A Mother's Farewell" by John Beaumont.
4. Ibid, "The Open Door" by Grace Coolidge.
5. Ibid, by Frances Greenwood Peabody.
6. Samuel Hinds, from *The Homebook of Verse* arranged by B. E. Stevenson.
7. A. L. Frink, *My Duty* (Clark Grave Vault Co., Columbus, Ohio), page 7.
8. Bret Harte, Ibid, page 8.

CHAPTER IX

1. Robert Richardson, *A Service Book* (National Selected Morticians, Evenston, Illinois).
2. Chauncey R. Piety, Christian Board of Publication.
3. James Dalton Morrison, op. cit., by Washington Gladden, page 592.
4. Charles L. Wallis, op. cit., by James Morrison.
5. Thomas, Curtis and Garrison, *Poems of Immortality* (Willet, Clark, Co., N.Y. 1935), poem by John White Chadwick.

6. Ibid, John Oxenham.
7. Robert Frost, *Collected Poems of Robert Frost* (Holt Rinehart and Winston, Inc.).
8. Chauncey R. Piety (Christian Board of Publication).
9. Andrew Blackwood, op. cit., page 154.
10. James Dalton Morrison, op. cit., page 592.

Poetry Index

Titles are listed in italics to distinquish them from first line references.

153

154

Index

Index of Aids
for Specific Circumstances